# Flower Farming for Profit

*The Ultimate Guide to Growing and Maintaining a Wildly Profitable Cut Flower Business*

AF866233

# BONUS

To kick start your foray into flower farming, I am pleased to offer an exclusive bonus for our esteemed readers. Simply access the link provided below or scan the QR code using your smartphone to be directed to our website. There, you'll gain access to a set of 8 complimentary templates designed to get your flower business up and running in no time.

www.myflowerfarming.com

# Table of Contents

# Introduction

"There is something infinitely healing in the repeated refrains of nature - the assurance that dawn comes after night, and spring after winter." - Rachel Carson.

The intoxicating scent of freshly cut roses, the vibrant hues of a sunflower field bathed in golden light, and the delicate petals of a peony unfurling in the morning sun are just glimpses of the magic that flower farming holds. Beyond the beauty lies a potentially lucrative and deeply fulfilling career, one where you cultivate not just blooms but a thriving business.

This book, Flower Farming for Profit, is your comprehensive guide to the exciting and challenging world of growing cut flowers for financial success. Whether you're a seasoned gardener yearning to turn your passion into profit or a complete novice drawn to the allure of fresh starts and fragrant fields, this book has all the knowledge and tools you need to transform your dreams into a blooming reality.

## Unveiling the Secrets of a Wildly Profitable Flower Farm

Gone are the days of romanticized notions of flower farming as a leisurely pastime. While the joy of nurturing vibrant blooms remains undeniable, building a truly profitable enterprise requires a strategic and informed approach. This book goes beyond the picturesque facade to explore the key pillars that underpin a successful cut flower business:

- **Cultivation Know-How:** Master the art of choosing marketable flower varieties, understanding their specific needs, and implementing effective planting, growing, and harvesting techniques, ensuring your blooms reach peak beauty and quality.

- **Market Savvy:** Navigate the ever-evolving landscape of flower sales, from identifying your ideal customers and pricing your products competitively to creating an easily identifiable brand and establishing profitable marketing channels.
- **Financial Acumen:** Understand the financial intricacies of your business, from developing a solid business plan and managing your budget to tracking expenses, maximizing profits, and achieving sustainable financial growth.
- **Operational Efficiency:** Streamline your operations for optimal productivity, from choosing the right tools and equipment to building efficient workflows and managing logistical aspects like harvesting, post-harvest care, and transportation.
- **Entrepreneurial Spirit:** Embrace the challenges and rewards of running your own business, developing resilience, adaptability, and a constant drive for innovation to keep your flower farm thriving in a competitive market.

More than just a guide, this book is your roadmap to success. Each chapter uncovers specific aspects of flower farming, providing practical strategies, actionable steps, and real-world examples to illustrate key concepts. You'll get insights from established flower farmers, access valuable resources, and discover the secrets to building a sustainable, profitable business that aligns with your values and aspirations.

## Flower Farming for Profit: Reader's Guide

Get ready to cultivate your dream flower farm. Here's a glimpse of the exciting journey that awaits you within these pages:

- **Chapter 1: Getting Started in Flower Farming:** Learn about the essential tools you'll need, explore greenhouse magic, master transplanting, and learn record-keeping secrets.

- **Chapter 2: Care and Maintenance of Flower Crops:** Master water management, ensure post-harvest perfection, implement quality control, and embrace waste-not composting.
- **Chapter 3: Marketing and Sales Strategies:** Build local love, host blooming experiences, develop captivating branding, and maximize your marketing ROI.
- **Chapter 4: Financial Management:** Track income and expenses, navigate debt, analyze profits, manage payroll, and handle payments efficiently.
- **Chapter 5: Sustainability and Eco-Friendly Practices:** Explore sustainable farming, embrace energy efficiency, compost and recycle, control water and erosion, and choose sustainable flower varieties.
- **Chapter 6: Scaling and Expansion** Evaluate readiness, explore financing options, consider satellite farms, and develop a data-driven expansion strategy.
- **Chapter 7: Managing Challenges and Risks:** Identify potential risks like pest outbreaks, supply chain disruptions, and industry-specific challenges, and learn crisis communication strategies.
- **Chapter 8: Customer Relationship Management:** Build strong connections, implement a CRM system, offer referral programs, and provide value-added services to retain customers.
- **Chapter 9: Technology and Innovation:** Harness the power of tech with automated irrigation systems, drones, and research initiatives and analyzing returns on investment.
- **Chapter 10: Legal and Regulatory Compliance:** Understand agricultural regulations,

worker safety rules, organic standards, land rights, and legal intricacies.

- **Chapter 11: Building a Strong Team:** Identify staffing needs, implement retention strategies, prioritize workplace safety, and cross-train for flexibility.
- **Chapter 12: Future Trends in Flower Farming:** Explore the rising focus on sustainability, organic farming, regenerative agriculture, and research advancements in floriculture.

This book equips you with the knowledge and tools to cultivate a thriving flower farm, where success blossoms alongside sustainability and a strong foundation for the future is created from the start. By the end of this book, you'll have the knowledge, confidence, and practical tools to transform your flower farming dream into a profitable reality.

This journey is not just about financial gain. It's about cultivating beauty, connecting with nature, and building a fulfilling business that reflects your passion. Are you ready to cultivate a wildly profitable flower farm? Turn the page and embrace the fragrant world of flower farming.

# Chapter 1: Getting Started in Flower Farming

"There is no better time than now to embrace the quiet beauty of a garden," wrote Audrey Hepburn, capturing the essence of the joy and fulfillment that flower farming brings.

However, before you take the first step toward your dream floral haven, there's groundwork to be laid, tools to be gathered, and knowledge to be gleaned. This chapter is your comprehensive guide to laying out the basics for your flower farming journey, from getting the right equipment to nurturing your first transplants and keeping meticulous records.

## Choosing the Perfect Location for Your Flower Farm

Choosing the right location for your flower farm is the foundation for a thriving, profitable business. It's time to pick the perfect canvas for your masterpiece. Before you get swept away by visions of colorful blooms, here are three key aspects to ensure your land sets your farm up for success:

### Unearthing the Good Stuff

Healthy soil is the lifeline of your flowers. Imagine them as happy kids needing the right playground – fertile, well-drained, and packed with nutrients. Here's how to assess your soil:

- **Soil Test:** This is your cheat sheet. Get a professional soil test kit to analyze pH, nutrient levels, and drainage. Based on the results, you can prepare your soil with organic matter like compost or manure to create the perfect growing environment.
- **Drainage is Key:** Soggy soil suffocates roots. Look for land with a gentle slope or create raised beds so

water drains well. Clay-heavy soil might need additives like sand or organic matter to improve drainage.

- **Know Your Sunlight:** Different flowers need different amounts of sunlight. Sunflowers bask in full sun, while shade-loving ferns prefer dappled light. Make sure that when you are selecting the flowers you want to cultivate you have the right environment in which to grow them, even if it means creating artificial shade areas.

## Selecting the Right Blooms

Not all flowers are created equal when it comes to profit. Consider these factors:

- **Demand:** Research local markets and trends to see what flowers are in high demand. Talk to florists, farmers' markets, and event planners to understand their needs.
- **Climate:** Choose flowers that thrive in your climate zone. This ensures predictable growth and avoids costly struggles with unsuitable conditions.
- **Care Requirements:** Consider your time and resources. Low-maintenance varieties like zinnias or cosmos are great for beginners. At the same time, more delicate blooms like peonies might require extra attention.
- **Seasonality:** Plan a mix of flowers that bloom throughout the year to ensure a steady income and customer satisfaction. Think about incorporating early spring bulbs, summer favorites, and fall stunners.

The following table provides a starting point for choosing flower varieties based on key factors influencing success in your flower farm. Research individual varieties check their e suitability for your specific climate and market demands.

| **Flower** | **Demand** | **Climate Zones** | **Care Requirements** | **Seasonality** |
|---|---|---|---|---|
| **Zinnias** | High | 3-11 | Low maintenance, drought tolerant | Summer and Fall |
| **Cosmos** | High | 2-10 | Easy to grow, self-seeds readily | Summer and Fall |
| **Sunflowers** | High | 3-9 | Full sun, needs staking, attracts pollinators | Summer and Fall |
| **Marigolds** | Moderate | 2-11 | Easy to grow, pest repellent, edible blooms | Summer and Fall |
| **Dahlias** | High | 7-10 | Tuberous roots, require staking, diverse colors & | Summer and Fall |

| | | | | |
|---|---|---|---|---|
| | | | forms | |
| **Gladiolus** | Moderate | 8-10 | Corms, require staking, tall & showy flowers | Summer and Fall |
| **Snapdragons** | High | 7-10 | Cool-season annual, tall & colorful spikes, attract pollinators | Summer and Fall |
| **Lilies** | High | 3-9 | Bulbs, require well-drained soil, fragrant blooms | Summer |
| **Peonies** | High | 4-8 | Herbaceous perennials, shade tolerant, require support | Spring |
| **Tulips** | High | 3-7 | Bulbs, early spring bloomers, diverse colors & forms | Spring |

| | | | | |
|---|---|---|---|---|
| **Pansies** | Moderate | 3-8 | Cool-season annuals, tolerate frost, diverse colors | Spring and Fall |
| **Lavender** | High | 5-9 | Drought-tolerant, fragrant foliage, attracts pollinators | Summer |

## Designing Your Floral Haven

Are you excited to arrange your floral stage? Here's how to design an efficient and productive layout:

- **Accessibility:** Plan pathways wide enough for easy access by equipment to all planting areas. Think about future expansion too.
- **Sunlight Optimization:** Group sun-loving and shade-loving flowers together in designated areas to maximize their potential.
- **Companion Planting:** Research companion plants that deter pests or attract pollinators, creating a natural ecosystem on your farm.
- **Rotation is Key:** To prevent nutrient depletion and disease in your soil, practice crop rotation by planting different flower families in the same spot each year.

Your flower farm is an investment in your passion and livelihood. Carefully choosing your location, selecting profitable varieties, and planning an efficient layout will lead you toward blooming success.

## Essential Tools and Resources for Your Flower Farm

Launching your flower farm dream demands more than just seeds and sunshine. Equipping yourself with the right tools and navigating the logistical side sets the stage for sustainable success. Ready to explore the key steps in greater detail?

### Budget and Financial Planning

Before diving into tool shopping, map out your finances meticulously. Consider:

- **Startup Costs:** Factor in essential equipment, seeds, soil additives, irrigation systems, and any anticipated labor needs. Research average costs for your area and desired scale to create a realistic budget. Include unexpected expenses like repairs or transportation.
- **Operational Expenses:** Account for ongoing costs like fertilizer, water, marketing, potential licenses, and taxes. Be proactive and factor in seasonal fluctuations in demand and resource needs.
- **Revenue Streams:** Decide your sales channels, whether farmers markets, wholesale, subscriptions, or a combination. Research their expected returns and tailor your production accordingly. Consider diversifying to mitigate risk and cater to a wider customer base.
- **Seeking Funding:** If needed, explore options like loans, grants, or crowdfunding to bridge the gap between investment and profit. Research eligibility requirements and interest rates carefully to choose the most suitable option.

### Permits and Regulations

Compliance keeps your farm running smoothly and legally. Thoroughly research:

- **Local Zoning Regulations:** Understand land use restrictions and any permits that might be required for operating a commercial farm in your area. Consult with local authorities or seek professional guidance to ensure you're fully compliant.
- **Business Licenses:** Depending on your sales model, you might need specific business licenses and tax registrations. Don't underestimate the administrative side. Start any application processes early and allow ample time for processing.
- **Environmental Regulations:** Familiarize yourself with any water usage restrictions or pesticide limitations in your area. Implement sustainable practices like water conservation and organic pest control wherever possible.

### Building Your Business Plan

A solid business plan is your compass, guiding your decisions and attracting potential investors. Consider these key sections:

- **Executive Summary:** Briefly outline your farm's concept, mission, and unique selling points. What makes your farm stand out in a crowded market?
- **Market Analysis:** Define your target customer base, explore the competitive landscape, and research projected demand for your chosen flower varieties. Understanding your market intimately is critical for success.
- **Production Plan:** Detail your flower varieties, growing methods, and projected timelines. Consider incorporating companion planting and crop rotation techniques which optimize yields and benefit your soil's health.

- **Marketing and Sales Strategy:** Explain how you're going to reach customers and secure sales. Will you participate in farmers' markets, build an online presence, or partner with local businesses? Develop a targeted marketing plan and budget accordingly.
- **Financial Projections:** Present your comprehensive budget, projected income, and future investment needs. Be realistic and transparent to build trust with potential investors or partners.

**Sourcing Materials**

Acquiring your floral essentials is the fun part. Here's a deeper dive into each category:

- **Seeds or Cuttings:** Choose reputable suppliers known for quality and disease resistance. Consider starting with smaller quantities to minimize your risk and test demand in your local market. Look for varieties suited to your climate and soil conditions.
- **Basic Tools:** Invest in high-quality, durable tools that will last through years of rigorous use. It includes shovels, trowels, hand pruners, watering cans, hoses, and pruning shears. Wherever you can choose ergonomic designs to prevent fatigue and injury.
- **Larger Equipment:** Depending on your scale, consider tools like wheelbarrows, tillers, or irrigation systems. Renting might be cost-effective for smaller farms, especially in the start-up stages. Look for used equipment options for affordability.
- **Farm Structures:** If needed, plan for greenhouses, cold frames, or raised beds to extend your growing season or protect delicate varieties. Consider the pros and cons of each option based on your climate and flower choices. Upcycled materials

can be a budget-friendly way to create essential structures.

Starting small and scaling up as your business grows is often wise. Prioritize essential tools and gradually add equipment as your needs evolve. Utilize online resources, connect with local farmer networks, and explore used equipment options to source materials cost-effectively.

## Setting Up Your Greenhouse (Optional)

While not every flower farm requires a greenhouse, it's an extremely useful structure to have to extend your growing season, protect delicate varieties, and control the environment for optimal growth. If you're considering this option, here's a breakdown of key steps:

### Building a Greenhouse

- **Location:** Choose a well-drained, sunny spot with easy access to water and electricity. Consider prevailing winds and snow loads when determining size and design.
- **Material Matters:** Decide on a budget-friendly and durable option like PVC pipe and greenhouse film, prefabricated metal structures, or more permanent glasshouses. Research local regulations and building permits before construction.
- **Ventilation is Key:** Proper ventilation is crucial for temperature and humidity control. Incorporate vents, fans, or automatic systems to prevent overheating and disease spread.

### Setting Up a Water Supply

- **Reliable Source:** Ensure a consistent source of clean water, like a well, municipal water connection, or rainwater harvesting system. Think about storage options like tanks or barrels to buffer against fluctuations.

- **Delivery System:** Plan an efficient irrigation system based on your greenhouse size and layout. Options include drip irrigation, overhead sprinklers, or hand watering for smaller setups.
- **Water Quality:** Monitor water quality, especially if using wells or rainwater, to avoid introducing harmful minerals or pathogens to your plants.

**Pest and Disease Management**

- **Prevention is Key:** Implement preventative measures like good sanitation, proper ventilation, and companion planting to naturally deter pests and diseases.
- **Organic Options:** Prioritize organic solutions whenever possible, like insecticidal soap, neem oil, or beneficial insects like ladybugs, to control potential outbreaks.
- **Monitoring Matters:** Regularly inspect your plants so you catch any signs of trouble early and can respond promptly with targeted organic or least-toxic methods.

**Planting Schedule**

- **Research and Planning:** Research the specific growing requirements and seasonality of your chosen flower varieties. Create a detailed planting schedule that considers germination times, transplanting needs, and harvest windows.
- **Succession Planting:** Utilize succession planting so you have a continuous bloom throughout the season. Plant new seedlings or seeds as earlier crops mature, maximizing your greenhouse's potential.
- **Climate Considerations:** When adjusting your planting schedule, factor in your local climate and greenhouse environment. Adjust start dates for seedlings based on your specific conditions.

### Preparing and Amending Soil

- **Start Clean:** Remove any debris, weeds, or previous crop residue from your greenhouse beds. Consider solarization techniques to eliminate potential pathogens in the soil.
- **Test & Amend:** Conduct a soil test to determine pH, nutrient levels, and drainage. Enrich accordingly with organic matter like compost or manure, following the recommendations of your soil test.
- **Raised Beds:** Consider raised beds for improved drainage and easier access, especially if your native soil is heavy clay or lacks organic matter.

### Fertilizing and Amending

- **Choose Wisely:** Select organic fertilizers appropriate for your specific flower varieties and soil conditions. Avoid overfertilizing, as it can harm plants and pollute water sources.
- **Compost Power:** Incorporate compost into your soil preparation or as a top dressing throughout the season for sustained nutrient release and improved soil health.
- **Monitor & Adjust:** Regularly monitor your plant growth and adjust your fertilization plan based on their needs. Be careful not to over fertilize because this can cause stunted growth or burnt foliage.

### Starting Seeds or Planting Cuttings

- **Seed Starting:** Follow the individual germination requirements for your chosen flower varieties, including temperature, light, and moisture levels. Utilize seed trays, starter pots, or a dedicated propagation area within your greenhouse.
- **Planting Cuttings:** If you're propagating from cuttings, ensure proper hygiene and follow the right

techniques for each variety. Make sure you have the ideal temperature, humidity, and rooting medium.

- **Transplanting:** Following recommended spacing guidelines, once seedlings or cuttings have developed strong root systems, carefully transplant them into your prepared greenhouse beds.

Starting a greenhouse is an exciting but complex task. Thorough research, careful planning, and consistent monitoring are crucial for success. Follow and adapt these steps to create a thriving environment for your floral creations to flourish.

## Transplanting and Nurturing Your New Additions

Transplanting seedlings or cuttings into your flower farm is a delicate dance. Get it right, and you'll witness vibrant blooms flourish. This section will guide you through the steps to ensure your transplants thrive.

### Monitoring and Controlling Environment

- **Temperature:** Avoid transplanting during harsh weather. Monitor daytime and nighttime temperatures, aiming for a comfortable range for your chosen varieties. Consider shading or row covers for protection in hot spells.
- **Light:** Different flowers have specific light needs. Sun-loving varieties need full sun, while shade-lovers prefer dappled light. Adjust your planting locations and provide temporary shade structures as needed.
- **Humidity:** Maintain optimal humidity levels, especially for delicate seedlings or cuttings. Use misters, humidity domes, or pebble trays filled with water to create a moist microclimate.

### Weeding and Mulching Practices

- **Weed Warriors:** Weeds compete for resources and harbor pests. Regularly hand-weed around your transplants, focusing on removing young weeds before they establish themselves.
- **Mulch Magic:** Apply a layer of organic mulch around your transplants (avoiding stems) to suppress weeds, retain moisture, and regulate soil temperature. Choose materials like straw, shredded leaves, or wood chips.

**Implementing Crop Rotation Strategies**

- **Disease Defense:** Planting the same flower varieties in the same spot year after year can deplete nutrients and invite diseases specific to those plants. Practice crop rotation by planting different plants in that place every year r.
- **Nutrient Balance:** Different flower families have different nutrient needs. Crop rotation helps maintain balanced soil fertility and prevents nutrient deficiencies.
- **Pest Control:** Certain pests target specific flower families. Rotating crops disrupts their life cycles, making it harder for them to establish themselves on your farm.

**Managing Organic Matter and Composting**

- **Soil Food:** Healthy soil is the foundation for healthy plants. Top up organic matter through compost, cover crops, or green manure regularly. It improves soil structure, fertility, and water retention.
- **Composting Power:** Composting kitchen scraps, yard waste, and plant debris creates nutrient-rich compost for your flower beds. Research composting methods and set up a system that works for your farm.

- **Microbial Magic:** Organic matter feeds beneficial soil microbes that help with nutrient cycling, plant growth, and disease suppression. Nurture a thriving microbial community in your soil for long-term health.

### Dealing with Common Soil Problems

- **Drainage Dilemmas:** Poor drainage can suffocate roots and lead to disease. If your soil is heavy clay, consider raised beds, adding sand or organic matter to your soil, or installing drainage tiles.
- **Nutrient Imbalances:** Soil tests reveal nutrient deficiencies or imbalances. Address these with targeted organic fertilizers or amendments based on the specific needs of your soil and plants.
- **Ph Challenges:** Most flowers prefer slightly acidic to neutral soil (pH 6.0-7.0). If your soil is outside this range, use amendments like lime (for raising pH) or sulfur (for lowering pH) to create an ideal environment.

Carefully monitoring your environment, implementing proper practices, and understanding your soil ensure your transplants thrive and reward you with a bountiful harvest of blooms.

## Growing Your Business with Records and Resources

Running a successful flower farm requires more than just a green thumb. It's about meticulous planning, smart marketing, and sound financial management. This section equips you with the tools to navigate these crucial aspects:

### Keeping Comprehensive Records

- **Record Everything:** Track planting dates, plant varieties, soil amendments, harvest yields, and pest control measures. This data becomes invaluable for future planning, marking successful strategies, and troubleshooting problems.

- **Invest in Software:** Consider user-friendly farm management software to streamline record-keeping, track expenses, and analyze your performance.
- **Learn from Experience:** Regularly analyze your records to identify trends, optimize your processes, and make informed decisions for future seasons.

### Joining Local Farming Networks

- **Connect with Peers:** Find local farming associations, online forums, or mentoring programs where you can connect with experienced flower farmers and share knowledge, learn from their successes and challenges, and build a supportive network.
- **Collaborate and Share:** Explore opportunities to collaborate with other farms on buying supplies, sharing equipment, or participating in joint marketing initiatives.
- **Stay Informed:** Stay updated on industry trends, new technologies, and regulatory changes through your network and relevant publications.

### Marketing and Branding Your Farm

- **Define Your Niche:** Identify your unique selling proposition. Is it organic flowers, locally grown varieties, specific flower types, or unique arrangements?
- **Craft a Compelling Story:** Develop a brand identity that will resonate with your target audience. Tell the story of your farm, your passion, and the values you represent.
- **Spread the Word:** Utilize online platforms, like social media, your website, and local listings, to showcase your flowers and connect with potential customers.

### Setting Up a Customer Management System

- **Organize Orders:** Put a system in place to track customer orders, preferences, and communication history. It ensures personalized service and builds strong relationships.
- **Loyalty Programs:** Consider rewards programs or subscription boxes to encourage repeat business and build customer loyalty.
- **Gather Feedback:** Actively solicit customer feedback to improve your services and understand you customer needs and preferences.

**Creating a Website or Social Media Presence**

- **Build Your Online Home:** Create a visually appealing website showcasing your flowers, farm story, and contact information. Optimize it for search engines to increase visibility.
- **Engage on Social Media:** Utilize platforms like Instagram and Facebook to share captivating photos of your flowers, connect with your audience, and run targeted ads.
- **Collaborate with Influencers:** Partner with local influencers to reach a wider audience and authentically promote your farm.

**Understanding Pricing Strategies**

- **Cost-Plus Pricing:** Calculate your production costs, including labor, materials, and overheads, and add a desired profit margin to determine your base price.
- **Market-Based Pricing:** Research the prices of similar offerings in your local market and adjust yours accordingly to maintain competitiveness.
- **Value-Based Pricing:** Consider the unique value proposition of your farm, such as organic practices or locally sourced materials, and price accordingly.

**Packaging and Presentation**

- **Invest in Quality:** Use attractive, eco-friendly packaging that complements your brand identity and protects your flowers during transport.
- **Creative Touches:** Incorporate personalized touches like handwritten notes, branded stickers, or seasonal touches to make your bouquets stand out.
- **Post-Purchase Care:** Provide clear instructions on how to care for the flowers to ensure customer satisfaction and encourage repeat business.

**Managing Cash Flow and Finances**

- **Track Your Income and Expenses:** Meticulously track all income from sales and expenses related to your farm operation. Regularly reconcile your accounts and monitor your cash flow.
- **Budgeting is Key:** Create a realistic budget for your farm, including projected income and expenses. Adjust your budget as needed throughout the season to maintain financial stability.
- **Seek Professional Guidance:** Consult with a financial advisor or accountant to optimize your financial management strategies and ensure compliance with tax regulations.

Building a successful flower farm requires dedication, continuous learning, and a passion for your blooms. By embracing these essential practices, you'll be well on your way to cultivating a thriving business that brings joy to your community and financial security to your endeavors.

**Chapter Takeaways:**

- **Plan and Budget:** Create a realistic budget and business plan to guide your investment and ensure financial sustainability.
- **Gather the Essentials:** Equip yourself with the necessary tools and resources, including hand tools,

irrigation systems, and potentially a greenhouse if your climate requires it.

- **Master Transplanting:** Learn proper techniques for transplanting seedlings or cuttings to ensure their successful establishment and growth.
- **Record Keeping is Key:** Track your planting dates, varieties, soil amendments, and harvest yields to gain valuable insights and optimize your future seasons.

With these foundational steps in place, you'll be well on your way to cultivating a flourishing flower farm that brings beauty, joy, and success to your life. The next chapter will dive deeper into monitoring water and irrigation, mastering post-harvest handling, implementing quality control measures, and transforming your flower waste into valuable compost. Get ready to dive deeper into the day-to-day tasks that will keep your blooms thriving and your customers returning for more.

# Chapter 2: Care and Maintenance of Flower Crops

**"A flower does not think of competing with the flower next to it. It just blooms." - John Wooden**

This simple quote embodies the essence of successful flower farming. Nurturing your blooms to their full potential requires meticulous care and maintenance. This chapter explores the essential practices that go beyond planting seeds and hoping for the best. You'll explore strategies for monitoring water needs, ensuring proper post-harvest handling, implementing quality control measures, and even transforming flower waste into valuable compost. By mastering these techniques, you'll cultivate vibrant, healthy blooms that bring joy to you and your customers.

## Monitoring, Maintaining, and Harvesting Beauty

The joy of a thriving garden is unparalleled. However, keeping those flowers vibrant and bountiful requires more than just sunshine and good vibes. It's about understanding your plants' needs and using the right strategies at the right time. Here are some proven practices to transform your garden from good to great.

- **Monitoring and Adjusting Water and Irrigation:** Ditch the guesswork. Invest in a moisture meter to understand your soil's hydration levels. Grouping plants with similar water requirements simplifies watering schedules. Adjust for seasonal changes. Underwatering stresses plants, while overwatering invites disease. Find the balance.
- **Implementing a Fertilization Schedule:** Fertilizer is plant food. Research your specific plants' requirements and choose a balanced fertilizer suitable for your soil type. Apply according

to the instructions, avoiding over-fertilization that harms plants and pollutes waterways. Consider organic options like compost or manure tea for a more sustainable approach.

- **Pruning and Deadheading Techniques:** Pruning encourages healthy growth. Learn the proper techniques for each of your plant varieties. You can pinch back young stems which will encourage branching or remove spent blooms to encourage further flower production. Deadheading also prevents unwanted self-seeding.
- **Staking and Supporting Tall Flower Varieties:** Tall beauties often need a helping hand. Choose sturdy stakes or trellises that match the plant's height and weight. Secure stems loosely to allow for natural movement, and adjust ties as the plant grows. Staking early in the process avoids damage from wind and heavy blooms.
- **Pest and Disease Identification and Prevention:** Early detection is crucial. Regularly inspect your plants for signs of pests or diseases. Knowing what you're dealing with helps you choose the right organic or chemical control methods. Consider companion planting to attract beneficial insects that naturally control pests, and prioritize good sanitation practices to prevent outbreaks.
- **Organic and Chemical Treatment Options:** Always prioritize using organic methods like insecticidal soap or neem oil whenever possible. However, for persistent problems, chemical options may be necessary. Follow label instructions carefully and prioritize treatments that target specific pests or diseases while minimizing harm to beneficial insects and the environment.
- **Mulching and Weed Control Methods:** Mulch is your garden's best friend. It retains moisture, suppresses weeds, regulates soil temperature, and

nourishes the soil as it decomposes. Choose organic mulches like shredded bark or wood chips, applying a 2-3 inch layer around your plants. Regularly hand-pull weeds to prevent them from stealing valuable resources from your precious blooms.

- **Harvesting Flowers at the Right Stage:** Knowing when to harvest is key to enjoying your blooms at their peak. Pick early morning when flowers are cool and fully open. Look for specific signs like color changes, petal firmness, or the presence of pollen. Proper harvesting encourages further blooming, so don't be shy. Cut those stems and enjoy the fruits (or rather, flowers) of your labor.

Gardening is a journey, not a destination. Embrace the learning process, experiment, and don't be afraid to ask for help. With these tips and a little TLC, your garden will flourish, becoming a vibrant oasis you cherish season after season.

## Mastering Post-Harvest Handling for Flawless Flowers

The journey of a flower doesn't end at harvest. Proper post-harvest handling is crucial for ensuring your blooms arrive at their destination looking fresh, vibrant, and ready to steal the show. It's time to unearth the secret elements that guarantee success, going beyond the basics to make the most of every step of the process:

- **Cooling and Storage Facilities:** Temperature plays a vital role in flower longevity. Invest in proper cooling facilities like refrigerated rooms or coolers. The ideal temperature range varies depending on the flower variety but generally falls between 33-41°F (1-5°C). Maintaining consistent temperature and humidity levels slows down respiration and prevents premature wilting. Even a slight temperature change has a big impact on vase life, highlighting the importance of precise control in storage facilities.

- **Flower Handling Equipment and Tools:** The right tools make all the difference. Use sharp shears or pruners for clean cuts that minimize stem damage, preventing the introduction of pathogens and ensuring optimal water uptake. Buckets filled with a holding solution (water with a preservative) should be readily available to prevent dehydration during processing. Consider investing in specialized tools like stem trimmers and bunching equipment for efficient handling, consistent stem length and minimizing waste.
- **Packaging for Different Flower Types:** One size doesn't fit all. Choose packaging that caters to the specific needs of your flowers. Delicate blooms like roses require sturdy boxes with individual sleeves for support, preventing crushing and maintaining petal integrity. Sturdier flowers like sunflowers can be bundled together with minimal protection. Proper ventilation within the packaging prevents moisture build-up and fungal growth. Innovative packaging solutions, such as those that incorporate ethylene absorbers or moisture-regulating materials, extend vase life by mitigating factors that contribute to flower senescence.
- **Transportation and Delivery Strategies:** Time is of the essence. Plan your transportation routes efficiently to minimize travel time and exposure to harsh conditions. Refrigerated trucks are essential for long-distance deliveries, regulating the temperature range and preventing heat stress. For shorter journeys, insulated vans can suffice, but ensure proper temperature control measures are in place. Partner with reliable transportation companies that prioritize temperature control throughout the journey. Invest in real-time

temperature monitoring technology for added peace of mind.

- **Inventory Management and Record-Keeping:** Implement a system for tracking flower varieties, harvest dates, storage locations, and even individual bunch or box identifiers. It ensures efficient stock management and traceability of any quality issues. It also allows for data-driven decision-making. Regularly monitor inventory levels and adjust your harvesting and ordering practices accordingly to minimize waste and ensure you have the right flowers in stock to meet customer demand. Utilize digital inventory management tools to streamline the process and monitor sales trends and seasonal fluctuations.

Master these post-harvest handling practices and continuously seek improvements through research and innovation. It'll ensure your flowers reach their destination in pristine condition, maximizing their shelf life, customer satisfaction, and ultimately, the profitability of your floral business. Every step in the process, from careful harvesting to meticulous delivery, contributes to the overall quality and value of your floral offerings.

## Quality Control Measures for Thriving Flower Farms

Beyond the beauty lies meticulous planning and dedication. In flower farming, achieving consistent quality requires a strategic approach. Are you ready to uncover the essential quality control measures to elevate your flower farm, ensuring vibrant blooms every season?

- **Dealing with Seasonal Challenges:** Mother Nature throws curveballs. Be prepared for unpredictable weather patterns by utilizing season extension techniques like row covers, greenhouses, and shade cloths. Research cold-tolerant and heat-resistant varieties that thrive in your specific climate. Proactive planning and adapting your practices based on seasonal forecasts are crucial for minimizing potential losses and ensuring a consistent supply of high-quality blooms.

- **Sustainable and Eco-Friendly Farming Practices:** Embrace eco-conscious methods that benefit your flowers and the environment. Put in place integrated pest management (IPM) strategies to control pests and diseases naturally, which reduces your reliance on harmful chemicals. Utilize organic fertilizers and compost to nourish your soil and promote healthy plant growth. Sustainable practices improve soil health and biodiversity. It also increases flower quality and yield, while reducing environmental impact.
- **Succession Planting for Continuous Blooms:** Don't let your flower beds lie fallow. Plan your planting schedule strategically, incorporating succession planting techniques. It involves sowing seeds or planting seedlings at staggered intervals throughout the season, ensuring a continuous harvest of fresh blooms. Research the ideal planting times and maturity periods of different flower varieties to create a blooming calendar that makes the most of your flower production and caters to customer demand.
- **Identifying and Addressing Common Flower Problems:** Knowledge is power. Familiarize yourself with common flower problems like pests, diseases, and nutrient deficiencies. Regularly inspect your plants, and learn to identify early signs of trouble. Implement preventative measures like crop rotation and proper sanitation practices. If necessary, go for organic control methods whenever possible, prioritizing the health of your flowers and the environment.

- **Soil Testing and Nutrient Management:** Healthy soil equals healthy flowers. Conduct regular soil tests to understand your soil's composition and nutrient levels. Amend your soil accordingly, providing the necessary nutrients for optimal plant growth and flower production. Composting and mulching helps improve your soil's fertility and structure, creating a thriving environment for your flowers.
- **Incorporating Cover Crops and Green Manure:** Give back to your soil. Plant cover crops during fallow periods. These nitrogen-fixing plants enrich the soil, suppress weeds, and prevent erosion. When tilled back into the soil, they decompose, releasing valuable nutrients that benefit your future flower crops. Studies at New Mexico State University have shown that incorporating cover crops significantly improves soil health, leading to increased flower yield and quality over time.

Implementing these quality control measures will help you cultivate a thriving flower farm that produces beautiful, healthy blooms throughout the season. Continuous learning, adaptation, and a commitment to sustainable practices are the cornerstones of success in flower farming.

## Sustainable Practices for Thriving Flower Farms

Flower farms are havens of beauty, but maintaining their vibrancy requires more than just sunshine and seeds. Sustainable practices are essential for nurturing healthy flowers ensuring the long-term viability of your farm and contributing to a healthier planet. Here are some key strategies that go beyond the blooms, fostering a thriving ecosystem and responsible resource management.

- **Composting Flower Waste:** Don't let those spent blooms go to waste. Composting flower trimmings, stems, and leaves transforms them into nutrient-rich fertilizer, reducing waste and replenishing your soil. Studies published in the Journal of the Science of Food and Agriculture have shown that compost application improves soil health, moisture retention, and nutrient availability, leading to increased flower yield and quality.

- **Beneficial Insects and Natural Pest Control:** Nature has its own pest control solutions. Attract insects like ladybugs, lacewings, and hoverflies by planting companion flowers and providing nesting sites. These are natural predators and help keep harmful pest populations down, reducing your reliance on chemical pesticides and creating a healthy ecosystem within your farm. Research conducted by the University of California, Berkeley has found that ladybugs alone consume hundreds of aphids per day, effectively controlling pest populations without harming beneficial insects or pollinators.
- **Crop Rotation for Disease Prevention:** Disrupt disease cycles. Implement crop rotation practices, planting different flower varieties in the same bed over successive seasons. This simple strategy prevents the buildup of soilborne pathogens that harm specific flower types, promoting overall plant health and reducing the need for fungicides. Crop rotation significantly reduces disease incidence in various crops, including flowers, highlighting its effectiveness as a sustainable pest management strategy.
- **Drought Management Techniques:** Water woes? Water-saving strategies like drip irrigation, which delivers water directly to the root zone, minimizing evaporation and maximizing efficiency. Utilize mulch to retain moisture in the soil and consider drought-tolerant flower varieties that

thrive with less water. Drip irrigation will save up to 50% of water compared to traditional sprinkler irrigation methods, making it a crucial practice for sustainable water management in flower farming.

- **Maintaining and Repairing Farm Infrastructure:** Regularly inspect and maintain your farm infrastructure, including greenhouses, irrigation systems, and fencing. Address minor issues promptly to prevent them from escalating into costly repairs. Proper maintenance ensures the smooth operation of your farm and minimizes downtime during crucial growing seasons. It's a good idea to have a regular checklist and schedule so nothing gets overlooked and all essential infrastructure components are inspected and serviced.
- **Equipment Maintenance and Safety Protocols:** Safety first. Establish and enforce safety protocols for all farm activities, including proper use and maintenance of equipment. Prioritize the well-being of yourself and your workers by creating a safe and healthy work environment. Safety training sessions for your team to ensure everyone is familiar with proper safety protocols and emergency procedures are vital.
- **Handling Emergencies and Contingencies:** Be prepared for the unexpected. Develop a plan to handle emergencies like power outages, severe weather events, or pest outbreaks. Having a contingency plan in place minimizes disruptions, allowing you to react quickly and effectively to unforeseen challenges. Include protocols for communication, evacuation procedures, and resource allocation in your emergency plan to ensure a coordinated and efficient response during any crisis.

- **Optimizing Workflow and Time Management:** Streamline your workflow, utilize task management tools, delegate tasks effectively, and prioritize activities based on urgency and importance. Consider investing in project management software or mobile applications to keep track of tasks, deadlines, and resource allocation. Time management tools will give you more time to focus on critical tasks, maximize productivity throughout the season, and reduce stress levels for yourself and your team.

By using what is available, you'll cultivate a thriving flower farm that produces beautiful blooms, with a healthy ecosystem, a responsible resource management, and that contributes to a more sustainable future for the floral industry. Sustainable practices are an investment in the long-term success of your farm, the well-being of your workers, and the health of the environment.

**Key Takeaways:**

- Monitor soil moisture and adjust watering practices accordingly to prevent under or overwatering.
- Implement proper post-harvest handling techniques, including cooling, storage, and packaging, to ensure flowers reach their destination in pristine condition.
- Take on quality control measures like seasonal planning, sustainable practices, and problem identification to consistently produce high-quality blooms.
- Transform flower waste into nutrient-rich compost through composting, closing the loop and enriching your soil.

Now that you've equipped yourself with the knowledge to nurture your flower crops, it's time to turn your focus to bringing those blooms to market. The next chapter explores effective marketing and sales strategies, guiding you through the process of connecting your beautiful flowers with eager customers. Turn the page and prepare to explore the exciting world of flower marketing.

# Chapter 3: Marketing and Sales Strategies

**"Marketing is no longer about the stuff that you make, but about the stories you tell." - Seth Godin**

In today's competitive landscape, simply growing beautiful flowers isn't enough. To thrive in the floral industry, you need to cultivate not just your blooms, but also your brand and relationships. This chapter unveils essential marketing and sales strategies to help you attract customers, build loyalty, and achieve sustainable growth.

You'll explore the power of building relationships with local florists, the benefits of hosting engaging farm tours and workshops, and the importance of crafting a captivating brand identity and packaging that appeals to your target audience. You'll also dive into the intricacies of managing your marketing budget and analyzing your return on investment (ROI) to ensure your marketing efforts are yielding the desired results.

## Building Relationships with Local Florists

From colorful bouquets to meticulously crafted centerpieces, flowers add a touch of beauty and emotion to every occasion. However, for businesses looking to tap into this flourishing industry, forging strong relationships with local florists is key. Whether you're a farmer's market vendor, event planner, or online entrepreneur, cultivating connections with these floral experts will unlock creative possibilities and mutual success.

### Cultivate Connections at Farmers' Markets and Local Events

Farmers' markets and local events offer a vibrant platform to showcase your products alongside fresh, locally sourced flowers. Partnering with florists allows you to:

- **Expand your Product Offerings:** Bundle your complementary products with beautiful floral arrangements, creating unique gift baskets or eye-catching displays that attract customers seeking a one-stop shopping experience. Offer locally-made honey alongside a bouquet of wildflowers, or pair fresh artisan bread with a vibrant centerpiece.

- **Cross-promote Each Other:** Collaborate on marketing efforts, leveraging each other's social media presence and customer base to attract new audiences. It could involve co-hosting giveaways, offering bundle discounts, or simply featuring each other's businesses on your respective platforms.
- **Tap into the Local Community:** Build trust and brand recognition by supporting local vendors and building a collaborative spirit. It strengthens your connection with the community and contributes to a more sustainable and dynamic local economy.

### Create a Thriving Subscription Flower Service

Subscription flower services are a convenient and popular way for customers to receive regular deliveries of fresh blooms. Partnering with a local florist allows you to:

- **Offer a Diverse Variety of Flowers:** Leverage the florist's expertise and established relationships with growers to curate interesting and exciting arrangements that feature seasonal blooms and locally sourced flowers. It ensures freshness and introduces you to customers who appreciate supporting local agriculture.
- **Benefit from their Floral Design Skills:** Partner with the florist to develop themed arrangements for holidays, special occasions, or simply to add variety to your subscription options. Their creative flair will elevate your offerings and delight your customers.
- **Reduce Logistical Challenges:** Offload flower sourcing, storage, and arrangement to the florist, allowing you to focus on marketing, customer

service, and managing the subscription aspect of your business. It frees up your resources and allows you to scale your offerings efficiently.

## Establish a Flourishing Online Flower Shop

If you're venturing into the online flower market, partnering with a local florist provides several advantages:

- **Fulfillment and Delivery:** Leverage the florist's established infrastructure for efficient order fulfillment and local deliveries. It ensures timely delivery of fresh flowers to your customers, reducing logistical headaches and maintaining customer satisfaction.
- **Expertise in Flower Care and Handling:** Ensure the highest quality and freshness of flowers by relying on the florist's knowledge and experience in proper flower care, storage, and handling techniques. It translates to longer-lasting blooms and a positive customer experience.
- **Access to a Wider Selection:** Partner with multiple florists to offer a wider range of flowers, catering to different preferences and budgets. It allows you to cater to a broader customer base and provide a more comprehensive selection of floral arrangements.

## Leverage the Power of Social Media Marketing

Social media platforms like Instagram and Pinterest are powerful tools for showcasing beautiful floral arrangements and promoting your services. Collaborate with florists to:

- **Create Engaging Content:** Feature stunning photos and videos of floral arrangements, highlighting the florist's creativity and your unique offerings. Showcase the flowers used in your subscription boxes, capture behind-the-scenes glimpses of the florist's design process, or feature customer testimonials.

- **Run Joint Giveaways or Promotions:** Partner on social media campaigns to attract new customers and generate excitement for both businesses. Offer discounts on combined services, host contests with floral arrangements as prizes, or co-create engaging challenges related to flowers or event planning.
- **Cross-promote Each Other's Accounts:** Increase visibility by sharing each other's content and encouraging followers to explore both businesses. It allows you to tap into each other's audience and reach a wider customer base.

**Email Marketing and Newsletters**

Building an email list allows you to nurture relationships with potential customers and promote your offerings. Partner with florists to:

- **Develop Co-branded Email Campaigns:** Offer joint promotions, share floral care tips relevant to your products, or announce upcoming events featuring both businesses. Leverage each other's expertise and reach a wider audience through a collaborative marketing effort.
- **Segment your Audience:** Tailor your email marketing efforts to specific customer segments, showcasing relevant floral arrangements from your partner florist. This personalization leads to higher engagement and conversion rates.
- **Leverage Each Other's Email Lists:** With permission, cross-promote each other's services to a broader audience, expanding your reach and potential customer base.

**Partner with Event Planners and Venues**

Event planners and venues require floral arrangements for weddings, corporate events, and other special occasions. Collaborate with florists to:

- **Offer Comprehensive Event Packages:** Bundle your services with the florist's floral design expertise to create attractive event packages. It could include catering, venue rental, photography, and customized floral arrangements, providing a one-stop solution for clients seeking a seamless event planning experience.
- **Develop Referral Networks:** Build mutually beneficial relationships with event planners and venues by recommending each other's services. It leads to increased business opportunities for both parties and establishes you as a trusted resource for clients seeking event solutions.
- **Participate in Joint Workshops or Consultations:** Offer joint workshops or consultations to showcase your combined services to potential clients. Exhibit your expertise, build trust with potential customers, and demonstrate the value proposition of your collaborative partnership.

**Support Local Causes and Initiatives**

Partnering with florists on charitable initiatives strengthens your community ties and builds positive brand recognition. Consider:

- **Donating Floral Arrangements for Local Fundraising Events:** Contribute to worthy causes by offering floral arrangements for auctions, raffles, or silent auctions. Showcase the florist's creativity while supporting a good cause.
- **Host Joint Workshops or Events:** Organize floral design workshops or events where proceeds benefit a local charity. It raises awareness for the cause and provides a fun and engaging experience for the community.

- **Volunteer your Combined Expertise:** Offer your services and the florist's floral design skills to beautify community spaces, such as parks, libraries, or senior centers. It demonstrates your commitment to social responsibility and strengthens your connection to the local community.

Building strong relationships with local florists unlocks a wealth of creative possibilities, enhances your offerings, and paves the way for mutual success. By working together, you leverage each other's strengths, expand your reach, and contribute to a thriving local ecosystem that celebrates the beauty and joy of flowers.

## Growing Your Flower Farm Business

Running a flower farm is more than just nurturing beautiful blooms. It's about cultivating a thriving business that connects with your community and shares the joy of flowers. Here are some key strategies to help you blossom, from engaging experiences to data-driven decisions.

### Hosting Farm Tours and Workshops

Open your farm gates and invite visitors to experience the magic firsthand. Farm tours and workshops offer a multitude of benefits:

- **Revenue Generation:** Charge a participation fee, creating an additional income stream that offsets operational costs and supports farm growth.
- **Brand Building:** Showcase your passion, expertise, and commitment to sustainable practices, generating trust and customer loyalty. By allowing visitors to witness the care and dedication that goes into growing your flowers, you establish a deeper connection with your brand and differentiate yourself from mass-produced options.
- **Community Engagement:** Connect with potential customers, educate them about the intricacies of flower farming, and build lasting

relationships. Farm tours and workshops provide a unique opportunity to share your knowledge and passion, encouraging local support and a sense of community.

### Partnering with Wholesale Retailers

Expand your reach and establish a consistent revenue stream by supplying fresh, locally grown flowers to retailers. Consider these key points when venturing into wholesale:

- **Building Relationships:** Network with florists, grocery stores, and other businesses seeking high-quality, locally sourced blooms. Attend industry events, connect with local businesses, and leverage online platforms to build partnerships.
- **Negotiating Contracts:** Establish fair pricing, reliable delivery schedules, and clear communication channels to ensure a successful, long-term partnership. Define expectations regarding flower quality, quantity, and delivery logistics to avoid misunderstandings and ensure smooth operations.
- **Maintaining Quality and Consistency:** Deliver consistently fresh, healthy flowers that meet the retailer's expectations. Invest in proper storage and handling practices to ensure your blooms arrive at their destination in pristine condition, upholding your reputation for quality and reliability.

### Offering Flower Delivery Options

Cater to diverse customer needs and enhance convenience by providing multiple flower delivery options:

- **Local Deliveries:** Partner with local couriers or offer a delivery service within a specific radius. It caters to customers seeking same-day or next-day delivery for special occasions or spontaneous gift-giving.

- **Nationwide Shipping:** Utilize established shipping services like UPS or FedEx to reach customers beyond your local area. Partner with reliable providers who specialize in handling delicate perishables to ensure flowers arrive fresh and undamaged.
- **Subscription Boxes:** Offer curated seasonal bouquets delivered regularly, creating customer loyalty and generating recurring revenue. It provides customers with a convenient way to enjoy fresh flowers throughout the year and creates a predictable income stream for your farm.

### Gathering Customer Feedback and Reviews

Customer feedback is a goldmine of valuable insights for growth. Encourage reviews on social media, your website, and platforms like Google My Business. Utilize this feedback to:

- **Identify Areas for Improvement:** Address customer concerns promptly and take proactive steps to enhance your offerings. Analyze feedback to identify common pain points and implement improvements in areas like product quality, customer service, or delivery experience.
- **Showcase Positive Experiences:** Share positive reviews on your website and social media channels to build trust and attract new customers. Highlighting positive testimonials will serve as social proof, convincing potential customers to choose your farm.
- **Personalize the Experience:** Tailor your offerings and communication based on customer preferences. Leverage feedback to understand customer needs and develop targeted offerings, such as specific flower varieties, bouquet sizes, or delivery options.

### Pricing Strategies for Success

Setting the right price is crucial for ensuring the long-term sustainability of your flower farm. Consider these factors when developing your pricing strategy:

- **Production Costs:** Factor in all expenses associated with growing your flowers, including labor, seeds, materials, equipment, and overhead costs. Accurately calculating your production costs allows you to set prices that cover your expenses and generate a profit.
- **Market Competition:** Research local flower pricing and competitor offerings to understand the pricing landscape within your market. While remaining competitive, avoid undercutting yourself and ensure your prices reflect the value you deliver through locally grown, high-quality flowers.
- **Value Proposition:** Highlight the unique qualities of your flowers, such as local sourcing, sustainable practices, unique varieties, or exceptional customer service. Communicate the value proposition that differentiates your farm from competitors and justifies your pricing strategy.

### Data-Driven Decisions

In today's data-driven world, monitoring key metrics is essential for understanding your business performance and optimizing your strategies. Track the following:

- **Website Traffic and Conversion Rates:** Identify which marketing channels are most effective in attracting customers to your website and converting them into paying customers.
- **Social Media Engagement:** Monitor metrics like likes, shares, and comments to understand which content resonates with your audience and adjust your social media strategy accordingly.
- **Sales Trends and Customer Behavior:** Analyze sales data to identify popular flower varieties, and

seasonal trends. Using this data will help you organize your inventory and plan your promotions, as well as give you a good idea of where your expansion opportunities lie.

### Implementing Seasonal Promotions and Discounts

Leverage the natural ebb and flow of flower availability to create excitement and encourage customer engagement:

- **Seasonal Specials:** Changing seasons are ideal times to feature flowers that are at their peak, and create some marketing excitement during these times. They highlight the beauty and variety of seasonal flowers and encourages customers to appreciate the fleeting nature of nature's bounty.
- **Early Bird Discounts:** Incentivize pre-orders for seasonal favorites by offering early bird discounts. It helps you gauge demand and secure orders in advance, allowing for better planning and resource allocation.
- **Clearance Sales:** Towards the end of a season, offer discounted prices on flowers that are nearing the end of their bloom cycle. It reduces waste, attracts budget-conscious customers, and creates a sense of urgency, encouraging quick purchases.

Implementing these strategies will transform your flower farm from a field of blooms into a thriving business that flourishes year-round. Success lies in cultivating strong relationships, embracing innovation, and making data-driven decisions that nurture both your flowers and your business.

## Branding, Marketing, and Customer Care for Florists

Standing out from the crowd requires more than just beautiful blooms in flower farming. A strong brand, strategic marketing, and exceptional customer care are essential for prospering in a competitive market. It's time for you to dive into these key areas and cultivate a thriving floral business that blossoms with success.

### Branding and Packaging for Marketability

Your brand is the essence of your business, encompassing your values, personality, and unique selling proposition (USP). Here's how to translate that into captivating branding and packaging:

- **Craft a Compelling Story:** Define your brand story, highlighting what sets you apart. Are you passionate about sustainable practices? Do you specialize in rare, exotic blooms? Communicate your unique narrative to resonate with your target audience.
- **Develop a Cohesive Visual Identity:** Create a consistent brand identity that reflects your story across all touch points, from your logo and website to your packaging and marketing materials. Utilize colors, fonts, and imagery that evoke the emotions and values associated with your brand.
- **Elevate your Packaging:** Invest in high-quality, sustainable packaging that complements your brand identity and protects your delicate flowers. Consider incorporating brand-specific touches, like personalized messages or eco-friendly materials, to create a memorable experience for your customers.

### Expanding Your Market Reach

Don't limit yourself to your local storefront. Explore these strategies to reach a wider audience:

- **Embrace the Digital World:** Develop a user-friendly website showcasing your floral arrangements, brand story, and ordering options. Utilize search engine optimization (SEO) to improve your online visibility and leverage social media platforms like Instagram and Pinterest to visually connect with potential customers.

- **Collaborate with Complementary Businesses:** Partner with local businesses like event planners, wedding venues, or gift shops to offer your floral arrangements as part of their packages or services. It exposes your brand to a new customer base and fosters mutually beneficial partnerships.
- **Participate in Industry Events:** Attend flower shows, farmers' markets, and other industry events to showcase your arrangements, network with other professionals, and gain valuable insights into market trends.

### Building a Customer Loyalty Program

Rewarding loyal customers, encourages repeat business and builds lasting relationships. Consider these options:

- **Implement a Loyalty Program:** Offer points or rewards for repeat purchases, encouraging customers to return and spend more over time. It incentivizes customer loyalty and provides valuable data on their preferences and buying habits.
- **Offer Exclusive Benefits:** Build up a members-only loyalty program with exclusive discounts, early access to new products, or special promotions. It creates a sense of exclusivity and appreciation, strengthening customer relationships.
- **Personalize the Experience:** Go beyond generic rewards. Offer birthday discounts, personalized recommendations, or early access to seasonal favorites based on individual customer personalities. It demonstrates that you value their business, understand who they are, and creates a more meaningful connection.

### Networking with Other Local Businesses

Building strong relationships within your community opens doors to new opportunities and collaborations. Here's how to leverage your local network:

- **Connect with Complementary Businesses:** Partner with local businesses that cater to similar clientele, such as photographers, caterers, or event planners. Cross-promote each other's services and offer bundled packages to attract new customers and expand your reach.
- **Support Local Initiatives:** Sponsor local events, donate flowers to charitable causes, or participate in community projects. It demonstrates your commitment to the community, fosters goodwill, and creates positive brand associations.
- **Collaborate on Workshops or Events:** Partner with other local businesses to host joint workshops or events related to flowers, crafts, or home décor. It's a fun and engaging way to attract new customers, showcase your expertise, and build stronger connections within the community.

**Participating in Flower-Related Events**

Industry events are valuable opportunities for professional development, networking, and brand exposure:

- **Attend Flower Shows and Trade Fairs:** These events showcase the latest trends in floral design, connect you with industry professionals, and provide opportunities to learn from experts and discover new products and techniques.
- **Compete in Floral Design Competitions:** Participating in competitions elevates your brand profile, showcases your creativity, and potentially leads to recognition and new business opportunities.
- **Host Workshops or Events:** Share your knowledge and passion for flowers by hosting

workshops on floral arranging, gardening, or flower care. It's a great way to connect with potential customers, establish yourself as an expert, and generate additional revenue.

## Managing Customer Inquiries and Orders

Providing exceptional customer service is crucial for building trust and cementing loyalty. Here are some key practices:

- **Respond Promptly and Professionally:** Ensure all customer inquiries are addressed promptly and professionally, regardless of the channel used. It demonstrates your commitment to providing excellent service, that you are professional and your customers are important to your business.
- **Offer Multiple Communication Channels:** Allow customers to reach you through a range of channels, such as phone, email, social media, or a live chat option, to answer questions, take orders and ensure accessibility.
- **Implement a User-friendly Ordering System:** Ensure your ordering process is clear, streamlined, and secure. Offer online ordering options for convenience and consider implementing a system that tracks order history and choices to personalize the experience for returning customers.
- **Go the Extra Mile:** Exceed customer expectations by offering personalized touches, such as handwritten notes or complimentary upgrades. Create a memorable experience and foster customer loyalty.

These strategies will cultivate a brand that resonates with your target audience, expand your reach beyond your local storefront, and build lasting relationships with your customers. Success in the floral industry lies in nurturing your brand, your marketing efforts, and the connections you build with your community.

# Marketing Strategies and ROI Analysis for Your Flower Business

In the vibrant world of flowers, aesthetics reign supreme. A strategic marketing approach is essential for blossoming success. However, navigating the world of marketing budgets and return on investment (ROI) is overwhelming when you're a beginner. Here are some key marketing strategies and practical tips to maximize your floral business's impact.

## Exploring Online Advertising and PPC

The digital landscape offers a fertile ground to reach new customers. Consider these options:

- **Targeted Online Advertising:** Utilize platforms like Google Ads and Facebook Ads to target specific demographics and interests with visually appealing ads showcasing your floral arrangements. Leverage precise targeting options to ensure your message reaches the right audience.
- **Pay-per-click (PPC) Campaigns:** Focus your advertising budget on clicks that convert into sales. PPC platforms like Google Ads charge you only when someone clicks on your ad, allowing for efficient budget allocation and measurable results.

## Public Relations and Media Outreach

Building positive relationships with the media amplifies your brand message and helps you reach a wider audience:

- **Develop Press Releases and Media Kits:** Highlight your unique brand, community involvement, or participation in industry events. Share these materials with relevant media outlets to generate press coverage.
- **Network with Journalists and Bloggers:** Build relationships with journalists and bloggers who cover your industry. Offer exclusive content,

product samples, or insights to secure positive mentions and reach their audience.

### Creating a Marketing Calendar

A well-defined marketing calendar ensures consistency and strategic execution:

- **Plan Seasonal Campaigns:** Make the most of holidays, special occasions, and changing seasons to create targeted marketing campaigns that capitalize on peak demand periods.
- **Schedule Social Media Posts:** Plan and schedule engaging social media content in advance to maintain consistent brand presence and audience engagement.
- **Track Key Dates and Deadlines:** Ensure timely execution of marketing initiatives by including important dates, deadlines, and budget allocations for each campaign in your calendar.

### Sales Forecasting and Inventory Planning

Accurate sales forecasting helps you optimize your marketing efforts and manage inventory effectively:

- **Analyze Historical Sales Data:** Identify trends and patterns in customer behavior to predict future demand for specific flower varieties and arrangements.
- **Consider Seasonal Fluctuations:** Adjust your inventory levels based on anticipated demand during peak seasons like holidays or wedding season to avoid stockouts or overstocking.
- **Partner with Reliable Suppliers:** Establish strong relationships with reliable suppliers to make sure they have timely access to fresh flowers and avoid disruptions in your ability to fulfill customer orders.

### Handling Customer Complaints and Returns

Prompt and professional handling of customer concerns builds trust and loyalty:

- **Implement a Clear Return Policy:** Outline your return and exchange policy clearly on your website and marketing materials to manage customer expectations.
- **Respond Promptly and Empathetically:** Address customer complaints promptly and with empathy. Listen to their concerns, offer solutions, and strive to resolve issues efficiently.
- **Go the Extra Mile:** Consider offering small gestures of goodwill, such as discounts or complimentary upgrades, to demonstrate your commitment to customer satisfaction. Never underestimate the effect this has on customer loyalty and word-of-mouth sales.

**Evaluating Market Trends and Demand**

Understanding evolving trends and consumer preferences is crucial for adapting your offerings:

- **Monitor Industry Publications and Social Media:** Keep abreast of emerging trends in floral design, color palettes, and popular flower varieties by following industry publications and social media discussions, and don't leave out home decor industry trends.
- **Conduct Customer Surveys and Focus Groups:** Gather direct feedback from your customers through surveys or focus groups to understand their preferences and identify potential areas for improvement in your product offerings or services.
- **Adapt your Offerings:** Based on your research and customer feedback, consider introducing new flower varieties, expanding your product range to

include gift baskets or home décor items, or offering unique services like floral subscription boxes.

### Expanding Your Product Offerings

Offering a diverse range of products attracts new customers and increases revenue:

- **Introduce Seasonal Arrangements:** Create spectacular arrangements featuring seasonal flowers to cater to changing customer choices throughout the year.
- **Explore Gift Options:** Expand your product offerings to include gift baskets, potted plants, or floral accessories to cater to diverse customer needs and occasions.
- **Consider Wedding and Event Services:** Once your farm is well established, consider offering comprehensive wedding and event floral packages, including bouquets, centerpieces, and venue decoration, to cater to a broader clientele seeking full-service solutions.

By strategically allocating your marketing budget, implementing effective strategies, and continuously adapting to market trends, you'll cultivate a thriving floral business that blossoms with success. The trick is understanding your target audience, delivering exceptional customer service, and creating a brand that resonates with the values and aspirations of your customers.

### Key Takeaways:

- Building strong relationships with local florists unlocks creative possibilities and expands your market reach.
- Hosting farm tours and workshops connects you with potential customers, allows you to showcase your expertise, and generates additional revenue streams.

- Developing a unique brand identity and investing in high-quality packaging is essential for standing out in a crowded marketplace.
- Effective marketing requires careful planning, budget allocation, and ongoing analysis to ensure your efforts are delivering a positive return on investment.

Now that you've explored the key marketing and sales strategies for your flower farm business, it's time to turn your attention to the financial aspects of your operation. In the next chapter, you'll discover essential financial management practices, from budgeting and pricing to recordkeeping and tax planning. Understanding these financial fundamentals will equip you to make informed decisions, achieve profitability, and ensure the long-term sustainability of your floral enterprise.

# Chapter 4: Financial Management

"Wealth is not about having a lot of money; it's about having a lot of options," said Suze Orman, highlighting the importance of sound financial management in any endeavor.

While the beauty and joy of flowers are at the heart of your farm, ensuring its financial stability is crucial for its long-term success. This chapter is all about the financial aspects of your flower farm, from tracking income and expenses to managing debt and analyzing your profitability.

## Tracking Income and Expenses

Running a successful flower business requires more than just a green thumb. Mastering your finances is crucial for your floral passion to blossom into a thriving and sustainable venture. It's time to explore some essential financial management strategies to navigate the world of budgets, cash flow, and financial planning.

### Creating a Detailed Budget

A well-defined budget is your financial roadmap. Here's how to create one:

- **List all Income Sources:** Include revenue from flower sales, workshops, subscriptions, or any other income your business generates.
- **Identify all Expenses:** Detail every expense associated with your business, such as rent, utilities, seeds, supplies, marketing costs, and transportation.
- **Categorize Expenses:** Group expenses into categories like operational costs, marketing expenses, and owner's compensation. It helps track spending in specific areas and identify potential areas for cost savings.
- **Set Realistic Projections:** Base your income and expense projections on historical data, market

research, and industry trends. Avoid overly optimistic estimates to ensure your budget reflects a realistic picture of your financial situation.

### Cash Flow Management

Cash flow, not just profit, is the lifeblood of any business. Here's how to manage it effectively:

- **Track your Cash Flow:** Monitor incoming and outgoing cash daily or weekly. It gives you real-time insights into your financial health and helps you identify potential cash flow shortages.
- **Manage your Inventory:** Keep your inventory at reasonable levels to avoid tying up cash in unnecessary stock while ensuring you have adequate supplies to meet customer demand.
- **Utilize Invoicing and Payment Processing Tools:** Implement efficient invoicing and payment processing systems to collect payments promptly and avoid delays that disrupt your cash flow.

### Setting Financial Goals

Financial goals provide a clear direction for your business. Here's how to set meaningful ones:

- **Define your Short-term and Long-term Goals:** Consider goals like increasing sales by a specific percentage, expanding your product offerings, or opening a second location.
- **Set SMART Goals:** Ensure your goals are Specific, Measurable, Achievable, Relevant, and Time-bound. It ensures clarity, focus, and a timeframe for achieving your desired outcomes.
- **Review and Adjust your Goals Regularly:** As your business evolves and market conditions change, revisit and adjust your financial goals to remain adaptable and responsive to evolving needs.

### Pricing for Profit

Setting the right price is essential for your business to thrive. Here's how to approach it:

- **Factor in all your Costs:** Calculate the total cost of producing and selling your flowers, including variable costs like materials and labor, and fixed costs like rent and utilities.
- **Understand Market Competition:** Research competitor pricing and market trends to determine a competitive price point while ensuring your prices cover your costs and generate a profit margin.
- **Consider Offering Tiered Pricing:** Provide various price points for different flower arrangements and product types to cater to diverse customer budgets and preferences.

### Tax Obligations

Understanding your tax responsibilities is vital for financial compliance. Here's what to keep in mind:

- **Identify your Business Structure:** Determine your business structure (sole proprietorship, LLC, etc.) as it influences how your business profits are taxed.
- **Consult a Tax Professional:** Seek guidance from a qualified professional to ensure you understand your tax filing requirements and comply with all federal and state tax regulations.
- **Set Aside Funds for Taxes:** Regularly set aside a portion of your income to cover your tax obligations. It helps avoid surprises come tax season and ensures you have the necessary funds readily available.

### Financial Forecasting and Projections

Financial forecasting helps you anticipate future financial performance. Here's how to leverage it:

- **Utilize Financial Forecasting Tools:** Consider using budgeting software or online tools to create financial forecasts that predict your future income, expenses, and cash flow based on historical data and assumptions about future growth.
- **Stress Test your Projections:** Assess the impact of potential economic downturns or unforeseen circumstances on your financial forecasts. It helps you identify potential vulnerabilities and develop contingency plans to mitigate risks.
- **Review and Update your Projections Regularly:** As market conditions change and you gather new data, update your financial projections to maintain their accuracy and effectiveness in guiding your financial decisions.

### Securing Financing or Grants

Financing fuels your business growth to the next level. Here's how to explore your options:

- **Research Loan Options:** Explore business loans, lines of credit, and other financing options offered by banks, credit unions, and online lenders. Compare interest rates, terms, and repayment conditions to find the most suitable option.
- **Consider Grant Opportunities:** Research grants offered by government agencies, non-profit organizations, or industry associations that support small businesses or businesses focused on sustainability or community development.
- **Develop a Compelling Business Plan:** If you're seeking financing, create a comprehensive business plan that outlines your business concept, financial projections, and growth strategies. It demonstrates your commitment to success and increases your chances of securing funding.

Implementing these financial management strategies will give you control over your floral business's financial health. Budgeting, cash flow management, and goal setting, coupled with a clear understanding of your tax obligations and a proactive approach to financial planning, will equip you with the tools and knowledge necessary to nurture your business and watch it blossom into a thriving financial success story.

## Managing Debt and Loans

Running a vibrant flower farm brings joy and beauty to your community but also comes with financial responsibilities. Managing debt and loans effectively is crucial for long-term success. Here are some practical strategies to keep your finances blooming.

### Implementing Cost-Cutting Strategies

Every dollar saved is a dollar you don't need to borrow. Here are ways to streamline your spending:

- **Conduct a thorough Cost Analysis:** Regularly review every cost associated with your farm, from seeds and fertilizers to equipment rentals and utility bills. Identify areas where you can optimize spending and consider negotiating better rates with vendors. Explore volume discounts, early payment incentives, or alternative sourcing options to reduce procurement costs.
- **Embrace Resourcefulness:** Explore alternatives to buying new equipment. Consider repairs, rentals, or bartering with other farmers to optimize resource utilization and reduce unnecessary expenses. Investigate the feasibility of shared services or equipment cooperatives with neighboring farms to spread costs and resources.
- **Utilize Energy-efficient Practices:** Implement sustainable practices like rainwater harvesting, LED lighting for greenhouses, and efficient irrigation systems to lower utility costs. Explore renewable

energy options like solar panels to further reduce your long-term reliance on traditional energy sources and their associated costs.

### Tailored Insurance Coverage

Be prepared for unforeseen circumstances by having adequate insurance coverage specifically tailored to your farm's needs:

- **Property and Casualty Insurance:** Protect your farm against losses from fire, theft, or weather-related damage. Evaluate your specific risks and adjust your coverage limits accordingly. Consider separate policies for your buildings, equipment, and inventory so that you are properly protected.
- **Business Interruption Insurance:** Cover lost income if your operations are impacted by events like natural disasters or power outages. Analyze your potential revenue loss during an interruption to determine the appropriate coverage amount.
- **Crop Insurance:** This gives you financial protection against crop losses due to weather events, pests, or diseases. Research different crop insurance options offered by the USDA and choose a plan that matches your specific crops and regional risks.

### Bookkeeping and Accounting Software for Efficiency

Embrace technology to streamline your financial management:

- **Invest in User-friendly Bookkeeping Software:** Utilize software designed specifically for small businesses to track your income, expenses, and inventory. These solutions often integrate with your bank accounts, allowing automatic transaction imports and simplified recordkeeping.

- **Consider Accounting Software:** For more complex financial needs, consider implementing accounting software that offers advanced features like payroll processing, financial reporting, and tax preparation assistance. These tools provide valuable reports and analytics that help you identify financial trends, track profitability, and make data-driven decisions.

### Hire an Accountant or Financial Advisor

Don't hesitate to seek professional guidance as your farm grows and your financial needs become more complex:

- **Consult an Accountant:** An experienced accountant helps you interpret financial reports, manage your bookkeeping, and ensure compliance with tax regulations. They also advise on tax strategies, financial planning, and debt management to optimize your financial health.
- **Consider a Financial Advisor:** A financial advisor offers personalized advice on managing debt, optimizing investments, and planning for your farm's future. They help you develop a comprehensive financial plan that considers your long-term goals, risk tolerance, and investment options to secure your farm's long-term financial stability.

### Keeping Records

Maintaining accurate and organized records is essential for financial management, tax compliance, and informed decision-making:

- **Document all Income and Expenses Meticulously:** Keep detailed records of every transaction, including receipts, invoices, and bank statements. It ensures accurate bookkeeping and facilitates tax filings. Consider implementing a system for electronic recordkeeping and document storage for easy retrieval and improved organization.

- **Organize your Financial Documents Systematically:** Develop a system for categorizing and storing your financial documents securely, allowing for easy retrieval when needed. Create folders for different categories like income statements, expense reports, tax documents, and loan documentation. Utilize cloud storage solutions or secure physical filing cabinets to ensure safekeeping and prevent potential data loss.

## Evaluating Return on Investment (ROI) for Informed Decisions

Track the effectiveness of your financial decisions and optimize your resource allocation with data-driven insights:

- **Calculate the ROI of Investments:** Regularly evaluate your return on investment (ROI) for any new equipment, marketing campaigns, or other significant expenses. It helps you determine if your investments are yielding the expected financial benefits and inform future decision-making.
- **Use Data to Inform Your Decisions:** Utilize the information from financial data and ROI calculations to guide your future financial decision-making and optimize your resource allocation.
- **Analyze Trends:** Continuously analyze financial trends, identify areas where you can improve cost efficiency or increase profitability, and adapt your strategies accordingly. By making data-driven decisions, you can ensure your investments contribute to your flower farm's sustainable growth and financial success. Identify areas for improvement and adjust strategies.

These practical strategies will help you effectively manage debt and loans, cultivate a financially healthy flower farm, and ensure your passion for blooms blossoms into a thriving and sustainable business. A proactive approach to financial management, responsible debt management practices and a focus on cost-effectiveness, will lay the foundation for long-term success and allow you to focus on nurturing your farm and its magnificent flowers.

## Demystifying Profit and Loss Analysis

For flower farmers, the vibrant colors and sweet scents are only part of the story. Behind the scenes lies the vital task of understanding your business's financial health, and a crucial tool in this endeavor is the profit and loss (P&L) analysis. Prepare to dive into the intricacies of P&L analysis, specifically tailored for the needs of flower farmers.

### Understanding the Basics

A P&L statement summarizes your farm's financial performance over a specific period, typically a month, quarter, or year. It categorizes all your income and expenses, revealing your overall profitability. Here's how it breaks down:

- **Revenue:** This section captures all the income generated by your farm, including sales of flowers, bouquets, arrangements, or any other products or services you offer.
- **Cost of Goods Sold (COGS):** This reflects the direct costs of producing your flowers, such as seeds, fertilizers, soil amendments, and labor directly involved in growing and harvesting.
- **Operating Expenses:** This section covers all other expenses incurred to run your business, such as rent, utilities, marketing, insurance, equipment maintenance, and administrative costs.

### Calculating Your Profit

The core principle of P&L analysis is simple. Subtract your total expenses from your total revenue. The resulting figure, your net income, reveals whether your farm operated at a profit (positive net income) or a loss (negative net income) during the analyzed period.

### Making Sense of the Numbers

While your net income is a crucial indicator, a deeper dive into the details of your P&L statement reveals interesting information:

- **Identify Cost Drivers:** Analyze your expenses to pinpoint areas where you can reduce costs, such as optimizing fertilizer usage, negotiating better deals with suppliers, or exploring energy-efficient practices.
- **Evaluate Pricing Strategies:** Compare your revenue with your COGS to assess the profitability of your different flower varieties or product offerings. It informs future pricing decisions and ensures you're adequately covering your production costs.
- **Monitor Trends:** Track your P&L statements over time to identify trends in your income and expenses. It helps you understand the impact of seasonal variations, marketing efforts, or new product offerings on your financial performance.

### P&L Data for Informed Decisions

A well-understood P&L statement empowers you to make informed decisions for your flower farm. Here are some ways it can be utilized:

- **Resource Allocation:** Allocate resources strategically, directing investments towards areas with the potential for higher profitability or growth.
- **Financial Planning:** Use P&L data to project future financial performance and make informed decisions about loan applications, equipment purchases, or hiring additional staff.

- **Benchmarking:** Compare your P&L metrics with industry averages or similar farms to assess your relative financial standing and identify areas for improvement.

### Seeking Professional Help

While P&L analysis is a valuable tool, don't hesitate to seek professional guidance, especially if your farm is growing or your financial needs become more complex. An accountant or financial advisor will help you interpret your P&L statements, identify areas for optimization, and develop strategies to improve your farm's financial health.

By understanding and utilizing P&L analysis, you'll gain valuable insights into your flower farm's financial performance, make informed decisions about resource allocation and strategic planning, and ultimately cultivate a thriving and sustainable business that blooms year-round. A data-driven approach to financial management is essential for navigating the ever-changing world of agriculture and ensuring the long-term success of your floral haven.

## Flower Farm Budget Template for New Farmers

This template is a starting point and may need adjustments based on your circumstances.

| Category | Description | Estimated Cost | Notes |
|---|---|---|---|
| **Startup Costs** | | | |
| **Land lease/purchase** | Cost of acquiring land or renting space | Varies widely based on location | |

| | | | |
|---|---|---|---|
| | for your farm | and size | |
| **Infrastructure** | | | |
| **Fencing** | Securing your farm perimeter | Varies based on length and materials | Consider recycled or used materials |
| **Irrigation system** | Providing water to your flowers | Varies based on size and complexity | Explore drip irrigation for water efficiency |
| **Greenhouse (optional)** | Providing a controlled environment for specific flowers | Varies greatly based on size and features | Consider cost-effective alternative s like high tunnels |
| **Tools and equipment** | Shovels, rakes, hoes, pruners, etc. | Varies based on specific needs | Look for used equipment or rentals |
| **Seeds and Plants** | Purchasing seeds or seedlings for desired flowers | Varies based on type, quantity, and source | Consider starting with small quantities and propagatin g your |

| | | | |
|---|---|---|---|
| | | | plants later |
| **Soil and Amendments** | Providing optimal growing conditions for flowers | Varies based on soil type and desired amendments | Research organic options and source locally if possible |
| **Ongoing Costs** | | | |
| **Labor** | Wages or self-employment income (if applicable) | Varies based on the size of the operation and the number of workers | Consider labor-saving strategies like attracting volunteers or interns |
| **Water** | Cost of water usage for irrigation | Varies based on location and water meter readings | |
| **Fertilizer and Pest Control** | Organic or synthetic products to maintain healthy plants | Varies based on chosen methods and application frequency | Research natural and preventative pest control methods |

| | | | |
|---|---|---|---|
| **Marketing and Advertising** | Promoting your business and attracting customers | Varies based on chosen channels (e.g., website, social media, farmers markets) | |
| **Vehicle and Fuel** | Transportation for deliveries, market visits, and farm maintenance | Varies based on vehicle type, fuel costs, and usage | Consider carpooling, fuel-efficient vehicles, or renting for specific needs |
| **Insurance** | Liability and potential crop insurance | Varies based on coverage and provider | Obtain quotes from different insurance companies |
| **Miscellaneous** | Unforeseen expenses, repairs, and incidentals | Allocate a contingency fund | |

**Metrics for a Blooming Business:**

Beyond the financial metrics, some key indicators point toward a successful flower farm:

- **Yield:** This refers to the number of flowers harvested per unit of area. A higher yield indicates efficient use of resources and land.
- **Flower Quality:** Customers pay more for high-quality flowers with vibrant colors, long vase life, and minimal blemishes.
- **Customer Satisfaction:** Positive feedback and repeat business are crucial for sustainable growth.
- **Reduced Waste:** Efficient harvesting, storage, and marketing practices minimize waste and maximize profits.
- **Sustainable Practices:** Implementing eco-friendly methods like water conservation, responsible pest control, and renewable energy sources can attract environmentally conscious customers and contribute to long-term success.

Keeping track of financial and operational indicators helps you make informed decisions, adjust your strategy as needed, and ensure your flower farm blooms into a thriving business.

## Managing Payroll

As your flower farm flourishes, you may reach a point where hiring additional help becomes essential. However, managing payroll is daunting, especially for first-time employers. This section explores some essential aspects of flower farm payroll, equipping you with the knowledge and tools to navigate employee compensation effectively.

### Understanding Wage and Hour Laws

Compliance with federal and state wage and hour laws is non-negotiable. Familiarize yourself with these key concepts:

- **Minimum Wage:** Ensure you comply with the federal minimum wage and any higher minimum wages mandated by your state.
- **Overtime Pay:** Employees who work more than 40 hours in a workweek are entitled to overtime pay, usually one and a half times their regular hourly rate.
- **Meal and Rest Breaks:** Understand and stick to federal and state-mandated meal and rest break requirements for your employees.
- **Recordkeeping:** Keep accurate records of employee hours worked, wages paid, and deductions made for taxes and other authorized purposes.

### Payment Methods and Frequency

Several options exist for paying your employees. Choose the method that works for you and your employees:

- **Direct Deposit:** This convenient and secure method electronically transfers wages directly into employees' bank accounts.
- **Paychecks:** Traditional paper checks can be issued, but ensure timely and secure distribution.
- **Payroll Cards:** Prepaid debit cards dedicated to receiving wages are an option but carefully evaluate any associated fees.

### Classifying Employees and Determining Pay Rates

Understanding employee classifications is crucial for accurate payroll processing:

- **Exempt vs. Non-exempt:** This distinction determines eligibility for overtime pay. Most farmworkers are classified as non-exempt.
- **Job Roles and Pay Rates:** Establish clear job descriptions and corresponding pay rates for different roles on your farm, considering factors like experience, skill level, and market competitiveness.

### Taxes and Benefits

Several deductions may need to be withheld from employee wages:

- **Federal and State Income Taxes:** You are responsible for withholding federal and state income taxes from employee paychecks and submitting them to the appropriate authorities.
- **Social Security and Medicare:** You are responsible for contributing your share of Social Security and Medicare taxes and withholding the employee's portion from their wages.
- **Other Deductions:** With the employee's written consent, you can deduct for health insurance premiums, retirement contributions, or other authorized purposes.

### Payroll Software and Professional Help

Managing payroll can be time-consuming, especially as your farm grows. Consider these options:

- **Payroll Software:** Utilize user-friendly payroll software for small businesses. These tools can automate many tasks, including tax calculations, deductions, and paystub generation.
- **Professional Payroll Services:** Outsourcing payroll processing to a professional service can save you time and ensure compliance with complex regulations.

### Tips for Effective Payroll Management

- **Develop a Clear Payroll Schedule:** Establish a consistent and predictable employee payment schedule.
- **Maintain Accurate Timekeeping:** Put a reliable system in place for tracking employee hours worked, either through timesheets, electronic timekeeping software, or a combination of both.

- **Communicate Clearly:** Provide clear and timely communication to your employees regarding their pay rates, deductions, and pay schedules.

**Resources and Support**

Stay updated on relevant regulations and access helpful resources:

- **The U.S. Department of Labor (DOL) Website:** Offers comprehensive information on federal wage and hour laws, including resources for small businesses.
- **State Labor Department Websites:** Provide information on state-specific wage and hour regulations.
- **Professional Organizations and Agricultural Associations:** May offer resources and support related to payroll management for flower farms.

By adopting these strategies and staying informed, you'll confidently navigate the world of flower farm payroll. Accurate and timely payroll processing ensures compliance with regulations and fosters trust and positive relationships with your employees, allowing your flowers and your business to continue to bloom.

## Financial Planning for a Thriving Flower Farm

Running a successful flower farm goes beyond nurturing beautiful blooms. It requires a keen eye for financial planning and strategic decision-making. The following financial aspects go beyond the basics, empowering you to cultivate a sustainable and prosperous floral business.

**Mastering Negotiation**

Building strong relationships with vendors and suppliers is vital for securing competitive prices and optimal service. Here's how to approach negotiations:

- **Research Market Rates:** Before you start negotiating with suppliers, research the market price of the supplies you need. It gives you a baseline for negotiating the best possible prices.
- **Leverage your Business Potential:** Highlight your farm's potential for growth and longevity to encourage suppliers to offer favorable terms.
- **Explore Bartering Opportunities:** Consider bartering your flowers or services in exchange for goods or services from other local businesses. It's a mutually beneficial strategy for all parties involved.

### Building Protection

Investing in comprehensive business insurance ensures preparedness against unforeseen events:

- **General Liability Insurance:** Protects against claims arising from property damage, personal injury, or other third-party losses caused by your business operations.
- **Property and Casualty Insurance:** Covers losses due to fire, theft, or weather-related damage to your farm, equipment, and inventory.
- **Crop Insurance:** Provides financial protection against crop losses due to weather events, pests, or diseases.

### Securing Your Future

Plan for your future financial security by establishing appropriate retirement accounts:

- **SEP IRA:** This solo 401(k) option allows you to contribute a significant portion of your self-employment earnings toward retirement with tax advantages.
- **Individual Retirement Account (IRA):** Traditional or Roth IRA options offer tax benefits

and contribute to your long-term financial well-being.

### Investing in Growth

Investing in your farm's infrastructure and equipment can lead to long-term benefits:

- **Research and Consider Cost-effective Upgrades:** Always keep your eye on new developments that could improve your production like energy-efficient irrigation systems, sustainable lighting solutions, or automated equipment.
- **Plan for Future Needs:** Anticipate future growth and potential expansion needs when making investment decisions. It ensures your investments continue to support your farm's development in the future.

### Planning for the Future

Planning for your retirement and the farm's future is crucial for a smooth transition and continued success:

- **Develop a Succession Plan:** If you plan to pass your farm onto future generations, create a clear and documented succession plan outlining ownership transfer, roles, and responsibilities.
- **Consider Professional Guidance:** Seek advice from financial advisors or estate planning attorneys to navigate complex legal and financial aspects of succession planning.

### Expanding Your Horizons

Anticipate future growth and plan your finances accordingly:

- **Conduct a thorough financial analysis:** Evaluate your current financial health, including income, expenses, debts, and assets. It gives you a baseline for financial projections and informed decision-making.

- **Develop a Business Plan for Expansion:** Create a comprehensive plan outlining your growth objectives, resource allocation, funding requirements, and projected financial performance. This plan is crucial for securing any necessary funding or attracting potential investors.

### Staying Ahead of the Curve

Staying informed about industry trends allows you to adapt and thrive in a dynamic market:

- **Monitor Market Research:** Subscribe to relevant industry publications, attend trade shows, and network with other flower farmers to stay updated on market trends, consumer preferences, and emerging technologies.
- **Analyze Potential Impacts:** Evaluate how these trends might impact your business and consider adjusting your products, services, or marketing strategies to remain competitive.

### Adapting and Adjusting

Regularly assess and adjust your financial goals as your business and market conditions evolve:

- **Review your Financial Goals Regularly:** Schedule regular reviews of your financial goals. It ensures they remain realistic and aligned with your evolving circumstances, aspirations, and what is happening in the market.
- **Be Adaptable:** Don't be afraid to adjust your goals as needed. Market changes, unforeseen challenges, or personal circumstances may necessitate adjustments to your financial roadmap.

### Securing Your Legacy

Planning your estate ensures the smooth transfer of your assets after your passing:

- **Consult with an Estate Planning Attorney:** Seek professional advice to create a will, trust, or other legal documents that outline how your assets will be distributed after your death.
- **Understand Tax Implications:** Be aware of potential tax implications associated with estate planning and consider strategies to minimize them.

Financial planning is an ongoing process, not a one-time event. A strategic and proactive approach, continuously learning, and seeking professional guidance will help your flower farm survive and thrive for generations. Dedication and sound financial planning will allow your floral legacy to bloom for years.

**Key Takeaways:**

- Track your income and expenses meticulously. Maintain detailed records of all your flower farm's financial transactions, including sales, costs, and investments.
- Develop a budget and stick to it. Outline your projected income and expenses, and monitor your progress regularly to ensure financial sustainability.
- Manage debt wisely. If necessary, explore loan options strategically, considering factors like interest rates, repayment terms, and potential impact on your cash flow.
- Analyze your profit and loss (P&L) statements. Regularly review your P&L statements to understand your profitability, identify areas for improvement, and make informed financial decisions.
- Manage payroll effectively. If you hire employees, ensure you comply with all relevant labor laws and regulations, factoring payroll costs into your financial planning.

- Handle invoices and payments promptly. Establish a system for sending and receiving invoices and payments efficiently to keep healthy financial relationships with suppliers and customers.

As you've established a solid financial foundation, it's time to explore how to cultivate an even more sustainable future for your farm. In the next chapter, you'll discover strategies for minimizing environmental impact, embracing responsible resource management, and fostering a thriving ecosystem for your flowers and beyond. So, turn the page and step towards a sustainable and flourishing flower farm.

# Chapter 5: Sustainability and Eco-Friendly Practices

"The Earth has enough for everyone's needs, but not for everyone's greed," Mahatma Gandhi wisely observed. As a flower farmer, you have the unique opportunity to cultivate beauty while nurturing the very environment that sustains your passion. This chapter unearths the essential practices of sustainable flower farming, empowering you to minimize your environmental impact and contribute to a healthier planet, all while ensuring the long-term success of your farm.

Small changes have a significant cumulative effect. Embrace the opportunity to integrate eco-friendly solutions into your daily operations and inspire others to join you in fostering a more sustainable future for flower farming.

## Implementing Sustainable Water Practices in Your Farm

Water is the lifeblood of any farm, but its scarcity is a growing concern for all agricultural sectors, including flower farming. However, implementing sustainable water practices doesn't just benefit the environment. It also saves you money and improves your farm's overall health. It's time to dive into practical strategies to reduce water usage and conserve this precious resource in your flower farm.

### Understanding Water Usage Patterns

The first step towards conserving water is understanding your farm's current consumption patterns.

- **Track your Water Usage:** Install water meters in key areas of your farm, to monitor water use and identify areas with high consumption.
- **Analyze the Water Needs of Different Crops:** Different flowers have varying water requirements.

Research the specific needs of your crops and adjust your irrigation practices accordingly.

**Smart Irrigation**

Traditional irrigation methods can be wasteful. Explore alternative approaches that deliver water directly to the root zone, minimizing evaporation and maximizing efficiency:

- **Drip Irrigation:** This targeted system delivers water directly to the root zone of each plant, significantly reducing water loss compared to sprinklers. Drip irrigation saves up to 50% of water compared to traditional methods.
- **Subsurface Irrigation:** This technique delivers water below the soil surface, further minimizing evaporation and reducing weed growth.

**Retaining Moisture and Suppressing Weeds**

Mulching your flowerbeds is a simple yet effective way to conserve water:

- **Apply Organic Mulch:** Cover the soil around your plants with a layer of organic materials like straw, wood chips, or compost. It helps retain moisture in the soil, reducing the need for frequent watering and suppressing weed growth, further minimizing water competition. Mulching reduces soil temperatures and conserves up to 30% of soil moisture.

**Utilizing Water-Saving Technologies**

Technology is your ally in reducing water usage:

- **Invest in Moisture Sensors:** These devices monitor soil moisture levels and automatically activate irrigation systems only when necessary, preventing overwatering.
- **Explore Rainwater Harvesting:** Capture rainwater using barrels or cisterns to collect and

store rainwater for later use on your farm. It reduces reliance on tap water and conserves this valuable resource.

### Beyond Technology

Sustainable practices go beyond technology. They require a shift in mindset:

- **Fix Leaky Faucets and Sprinklers Promptly:** Even small leaks waste significant amounts of water over time. Address any leaks promptly to prevent unnecessary water loss.
- **Educate your Team:** Inform your team members about the importance of water conservation and encourage them to be water conscious in their daily tasks.

These strategies will significantly reduce your farm's water footprint, contribute to environmental sustainability, and potentially save money on water bills. Start implementing these practices today and watch your flower farm flourish and become a champion for water conservation.

## Energy-Efficient Practices in Your Flower Farm

Running a successful flower farm goes beyond nurturing beautiful blooms. It requires a commitment to sustainability. Being energy efficient benefits the environment and helps you save money on operational costs. Here are some practical strategies to cultivate a greener and more efficient flower farm.

### Nurturing the Foundation

Healthy soil is the cornerstone of any sustainable farming practice. Here's how to cultivate a thriving foundation for your flowers:

- **Composting:** Turn food scraps, yard waste, and other organic materials into nutrient-rich compost. It reduces waste and improves soil structure, fertility, and water retention, potentially reducing the need for additional fertilizers and irrigation.

- **Practice Cover Cropping:** Plant cover crops between flower seasons. These additional plants suppress weeds, prevent soil erosion, and fix nitrogen in the soil, improving its condition and reducing your reliance on synthetic fertilizers.

### Minimizing Waste

Reducing waste is not just environmentally responsible but also saves you money on disposal and management costs:

- **Rethink Packaging:** Explore reusable alternatives like cloth bags or biodegradable materials for packaging and delivering your flowers. It will significantly reduce your reliance on single-use plastics and contribute to a more sustainable floral business model.
- **Implement Recycling Programs:** Establish a system for collecting and recycling plastic pots, plant tags, and other recyclable materials used on your farm. It minimizes waste sent to landfills and contributes to a circular economy.

### Supporting the Ecosystem

A biodiverse farm ecosystem benefits both your flowers and the environment:

- **Plant Pollinator-Friendly Flowers:** Include a variety of flowering plants that attract bees, butterflies, and other beneficial insects. These pollinators ensure healthy flower production, reducing your reliance on hand pollination methods.
- **Create Wildlife-Friendly Habitats:** Provide nesting sites for birds and other beneficial creatures by planting hedges, creating small ponds, or installing birdhouses. It encourages a diverse

ecosystem that naturally controls pests and promotes the health of your flowers.

### Exploring Renewable Energy Options

Renewable energy sources will power your farm efficiently and sustainably:

- **Invest in Solar Panels:** Consider installing solar panels to generate electricity for your farm's operations. It will significantly reduce your reliance on traditional energy sources and contribute to a lower carbon footprint.
- **Explore Wind Power:** Depending on your location and wind resources, wind turbines could be a viable option for generating clean energy depending on your location and wind patterns.

### Optimizing Equipment and Practices

Simple adjustments in your daily operations lead to significant energy savings:

- **Maintain Equipment Regularly:** Regularly service your farm equipment to ensure it operates efficiently and minimizes energy consumption.
- **Utilize Energy-efficient Lighting:** When possible, switch to LED lights in your greenhouses and other farm buildings. LEDs offer superior energy efficiency compared to traditional incandescent or fluorescent bulbs.

Embracing energy-efficient practices and nurturing your soil and ecosystem will ensure your blooms flourish while minimizing environmental impact and potentially reducing operational costs.

## Composting and Recycling

As a flower farmer, nurturing beautiful blooms goes hand in hand with a healthy environment. Composting and recycling offer practical solutions to reduce waste, promote soil health, and cultivate a more sustainable floral business. It's time to explore how these practices empower you to grow stunning flowers while minimizing your environmental impact.

### Embracing Composting

Composting transforms organic waste into nutrient-rich "black gold" for your flower beds:

- **Compost Kitchen Scraps:** Instead of throwing away vegetable peels, coffee grounds, and eggshells, add them to your compost pile. Yard trimmings, such as leaves and grass clippings, can also be composted.
- **Benefits for your Flowers:** Composted soil improves drainage and water retention, promotes beneficial microbial activity, and provides essential nutrients for your flowers, reducing the need for chemical fertilizers. Compost will increase crop yields by up to 20%.

### Rethink and Reduce

Reducing waste at the source is crucial for a sustainable farm:

- **Rethink Packaging:** Explore reusable alternatives such as cloth bags or biodegradable materials for packaging and delivering your flowers. It minimizes plastic waste and is a more responsible floral business model.
- **Recycle Diligently:** Implement a system for collecting and recycling plastic pots, plant tags, and other recyclable materials used on your farm. It reduces your reliance on landfills and contributes to a circular economy.

### Minimizing Pesticides

Healthy soil and a diverse ecosystem are your allies in pest control:

- **Promote Biodiversity:** Attract beneficial insects like ladybugs and lacewings by planting flowers that provide them with food and shelter. These natural predators help control harmful pest populations.
- **Utilize Organic Methods:** Opt for organic pest control methods like neem oil or insecticidal soap when necessary. These natural alternatives are less harmful to the environment and beneficial insects than traditional chemical pesticides.

### Implementing Regenerative Agriculture

Regenerative agriculture focuses on building healthy soil and fostering a thriving ecosystem:

- **Minimize Soil Disturbance:** Practices like no-till farming can help maintain soil structure, promote microbial activity, and improve water retention. It will lead to healthier plants and potentially reduced water needs.
- **Rotate Crops:** Planting different types of flowers in your beds throughout the season helps prevent nutrient depletion and discourages pests that thrive on specific crops.

## Reducing Your Flower Farm's Carbon Footprint

As a flower farmer, you contribute to the beauty and vibrancy of your community. However, with great beauty comes the great responsibility of minimizing environmental impact. Here are some practical strategies to reduce your farm's carbon footprint, ensuring your flowers flourish alongside a healthy planet.

### Eco-Friendly Packaging

Packaging plays a crucial role in getting your flowers to your customers, but it shouldn't come at the cost of the environment:

- **Embrace Biodegradable Materials:** Choose for packaging made from recycled paper, cardboard, or plant-based materials that decompose naturally, minimizing waste sent to landfills. Look for certifications like the Forest Stewardship Council (FSC) to ensure the materials come from responsibly managed forests.
- **Minimize Unnecessary Packaging:** Avoid excessive packaging. Use appropriately sized boxes and use reusable elements like cloth wraps or baskets for local deliveries. Encourage customers to return or reuse them, further reducing environmental impact.

**Supporting Your Community and Reducing Emissions**

Sourcing local materials and partnering with nearby businesses will also reduce your carbon footprint:

- **Source Locally:** Whenever possible, purchase supplies, flowers, and other materials from local vendors. It cuts down transportation distances and associated carbon emissions. Look for local farmers who share your commitment to sustainable practices to create a collaborative and resilient local floral ecosystem.
- **Collaborate with Local Businesses:** Explore partnerships with local businesses for services like delivering your arrangements. Partner with local florists to offer farm-to-florist options, reducing the need for long-distance transportation and supporting other businesses in your community. It reduces transportation needs, strengthens your connection to your community, and builds a collaborative floral network.

**Conservation on the Farm**

Simple changes within your farm's operations will make a big difference:

- **Implement Water Conservation Practices:** Utilize drip irrigation systems, mulch your flowerbeds, and capture rainwater to reduce water usage and minimize the energy required for pumping and treatment. Explore water-efficient irrigation technologies like smart controllers or moisture sensors that optimize water delivery based on real-time needs.
- **Embrace Renewable Energy:** Explore options like solar panels or wind turbines to generate clean energy for your farm. It reduces reliance on fossil fuels and lowers your carbon footprint. Conduct a feasibility study to determine the most suitable renewable energy option for your specific location and energy needs.
- **Promote Healthy Soil:** Implement regenerative agricultural practices like no-till farming and cover cropping. It improves soil health, increases carbon sequestration, and potentially reduces fertilizer needs, further mitigating your environmental impact. Research and adopt cover crop mixes that attract and support beneficial insects, promoting biodiversity and natural pest control within your ecosystem.

Regardless of how small, every step towards sustainability contributes to a healthier planet and a brighter future for your blooms and your community. As you navigate this journey, continuously educate yourself on new sustainable practices, seek expert guidance, and share your knowledge with other farmers.

## Controlling Water Runoff and Erosion in Your Flower Farm

As a flower farmer, you understand the importance of water. However, uncontrolled water runoff and soil erosion can threaten your soil health, pollute waterways, and ultimately harm your business. Here are some practical solutions and strategies to ensure your beautiful flowers thrive in a healthy environment.

### Harnessing the Power of Nature

Switching to renewable energy sources will significantly reduce your reliance on fossil fuels and contribute to a cleaner environment:

- **Explore Solar Power:** Install solar panels on your farm buildings to generate clean electricity for your operations. It reduces dependence on conventional energy sources and minimizes your carbon footprint, contributing to a healthier ecosystem for your flowers and surrounding environment.
- **Consider Wind Power:** Depending on your location and wind weather, wind turbines could be a viable option for generating clean energy. This renewable source can power your irrigation systems, greenhouses, and other farm operations, reducing environmental impact.

### Education and Awareness Efforts

Spreading knowledge about sustainable practices is crucial for a collective environmental impact:

- **Educate your Team:** Train your employees on the importance of water conservation and erosion control practices. It empowers them to make conscious choices in their daily tasks and contributes to the farm's sustainability goals.
- **Engage your Community:** Organize workshops, demonstrations, or open farm days to educate your community about the environmental impact of flower farming and showcase your commitment to sustainable practices. It fosters awareness and encourages responsible consumer choices, potentially attracting customers who value eco-friendly values.

### Sustainability Certifications

Obtaining sustainability certifications demonstrates your dedication to environmental responsibility and offers several benefits:

- **Choose Relevant Certifications:** Research and pursue certifications aligned with your farm's practices and local context. Examples include Certified Organic, Certified Naturally Grown, or Salmon-Safe. These certifications will enhance your brand image, attract environmentally conscious customers, and potentially open doors to new market opportunities.
- **Maintain Transparency:** Be transparent about your sustainability efforts and certifications. Share your journey with your customers and community through your website, social media platforms, and marketing materials. It encourages trust and strengthens your position as a responsible and environmentally conscious flower grower.

**Beyond the strategies mentioned above, consider:**

- **Maintaining Buffer Strips:** Plant trees, shrubs, or grasses along waterways and around your farm's perimeter. These buffer strips act as natural filters, absorbing excess water and preventing soil erosion from entering waterways.

Embracing renewable energy, fostering education and awareness, and pursuing sustainability certifications will make you a leader in eco-friendly flower farming. Even small changes significantly impact your environmental footprint and contribute to a future where beautiful blooms flourish alongside a thriving planet.

## Choosing Sustainable Flowers for Your Farm

Your colorful blooms bring joy to countless occasions. Choosing sustainable flower varieties is an important step in this journey. It's time to explore ways to select flowers that flourish on your farm and contribute to a healthier planet.

### Conducting Environmental Impact Assessments

Understanding the environmental impact of different flower varieties empowers informed decision-making:

- **Research Water Needs:** Choose flowers with lower water requirements, especially in drought-prone regions. Landscape irrigation accounts for nearly one-third of residential water use in the US. Selecting drought-tolerant varieties will significantly minimize your water footprint.
- **Consider Pesticide Use:** Opt for naturally pest-resistant varieties or those requiring minimal pesticide applications. It reduces harm to beneficial insects and pollinators and protects the health of your soil and surrounding ecosystem.

### Collaborating with Environmental Organizations

Collaborate with environmental organizations for guidance and support:

- **Seek Expert Advice:** Partner with local or national environmental organizations specializing in sustainable agriculture. They will offer valuable insights into choosing sustainable flower varieties, implementing best practices, and navigating the ever-evolving landscape of eco-friendly farming.
- **Explore Certification Options:** Explore flower variety certifications that indicate environmentally responsible growing practices. Examples include the California Cut Flower Commission's "California Grown" certification or The Greener Flower's "Certified American Grown" program. These certifications will guide your selection process and potentially open doors to new market opportunities.

### Connect with Your Customers

Transparency fosters trust and strengthens your brand image:

- **Showcase your Commitment:** Educate your customers about your dedication to sustainable practices and the flower varieties you've chosen. Highlight the environmental benefits associated with your choices and the positive impact you're making.
- **Embrace Storytelling:** Share your sustainability journey through blog posts, social media content, or your website. Showcase the beauty of your flowers alongside the efforts you undertake to ensure their sustainable cultivation. It educates your customers and inspires others to embrace eco-friendly practices.

Choosing sustainable flower varieties goes beyond aesthetics. It's a conscious decision to nurture a thriving ecosystem alongside your blooms. Conduct environmental impact assessments, partner with environmental organizations, and share your sustainability story.

**Key Takeaways:**

- Explore and implement sustainable farming methods. Consider practices like crop rotation, integrated pest management, and water conservation techniques to minimize your environmental footprint.
- Embrace energy-efficient practices. Invest in energy-saving tools and equipment, utilize renewable energy sources whenever possible, and conserve energy through simple yet effective measures.
- Composting is key. Transform flower waste and other organic materials into nutrient-rich compost, minimizing waste and enriching your soil naturally.

- Reduce your carbon footprint. Explore ways to minimize your reliance on fossil fuels, and consider carbon offset programs to mitigate your unavoidable emissions.
- Control water runoff and erosion. Implement mulching, cover cropping, and proper irrigation practices to protect your soil and waterways.
- Choose sustainable flower varieties. Opt for varieties known for their low water requirements, resistance to pests and diseases, and suitability for your local climate.

By embracing these sustainable practices, you'll nurture the very foundation of your business and the well-being of the planet for generations to come. As you move forward, the possibilities for growth and expansion are limitless. In the next chapter, you'll explore strategies for strategically growing your flower farm, maximizing your profits, and taking your floral passion to exciting new heights.

# Chapter 6: Scaling and Expansion

"The only limit to our realization of tomorrow will be our doubts of today," Franklin D. Roosevelt remarked, capturing the essence of the potential that lies within each of us. The desire to expand and reach new heights might naturally blossom as your flower farm thrives. This chapter equips you with the essential tools to assess your readiness for growth, explore financing options, and strategize for sustainable expansion, ensuring your floral dreams take root and flourish beyond your initial borders.

## Assessing Your Flower Business for Expansion

The sweet scent of success hangs heavy in the air. Your flower business is flourishing. However, with every successful bloom comes the exciting question. Are you ready to expand?

Expansion isn't just about increasing your flower production. It's a strategic leap requiring careful preparation. Here are some tools to assess your business's readiness for growth, focusing on three key areas:

### Identifying Growth Opportunities

Look beyond the obvious. While increasing production often comes to mind first, consider alternative avenues for growth:

- **Specialty Offerings:** Dive into niche markets like wedding flowers, event décor, or even funeral arrangements. Researching consumer trends and local demand will help you identify profitable specialty niches.
- **Value-added Services:** Elevate your offerings by providing services like bouquet subscriptions, workshops, or floral design consultations. It'll increase customer engagement and brand loyalty.
- **E-commerce Expansion:** In today's digital world, establishing an online presence is crucial. Create a user-friendly website or leverage online

marketplaces to reach a wider audience. E-commerce sales have consistently grown over the past decade, indicating the vast potential of online flower sales.

## Increasing Flower Production

Scaling production requires a well-thought-out plan:

- **Resource Assessment:** Evaluate your current resources, including land, greenhouse space, labor force, and equipment. Are there areas where you can optimize what you have before investing in expansion?
- **Technology Integration:** Explore automation solutions like irrigation systems or temperature controls to streamline processes and increase efficiency. Understand and utilize automation to enhance agricultural productivity.
- **Sustainable Practices:** Consider including sustainable practices like water-efficient irrigation or natural pest control. Not only are these practices environmentally friendly, but they also lead to cost savings in the long run.

## Reaching New Markets

Don't limit your blooms to a single patch. Expand your reach by:

- **Identifying new Customer Segments:** Explore B2B opportunities like supplying hotels, restaurants, malls or event venues. Researching local businesses and understanding their needs opens doors to new partnerships.
- **Geographical Expansion:** Consider entering new markets with a growing demand for flowers. Analyze regional trends and identify areas with potential for profitable expansion.

- **Building Strategic Partnerships:** Collaborate with complementary businesses like florists, wedding planners, or event organizers. It'll help you tap into new customer bases and expand your brand awareness.

Expansion is a journey, not a destination. By carefully assessing your readiness and implementing a well-defined plan, you'll transform your flower business from a thriving garden into a flourishing landscape. Take a deep breath, nurture your vision, and watch your business bloom.

## Financing Your Flower Farm's Growth Initiatives

Your flower farm is a blossoming success, but your vision stretches beyond the horizon. Scaling up, however, necessitates capital, and understanding how to finance your growth initiatives is the key to nurturing your ambitions. It's time to examine various funding options to empower your floral aspirations, exploring areas like:

- **Small Business Administration (SBA) Loans:** The SBA offers a bouquet of loan programs designed for small businesses, including options tailored for hiring and training new employees. These loans often boast favorable terms and can be a great way to cultivate the skilled workforce you need for expansion.
- **Equipment Financing:** Several lenders offer specialized loans or leases for acquiring equipment like greenhouses, irrigation systems, or climate control technology. This targeted financing allows you to invest in the infrastructure necessary to expand your growing space and cultivate a wider variety of blooms.
- **Lines of Credit:** A line of credit provides the flexibility of a blooming flower bed. It allows you to access funds as needed, which is perfect for purchasing seeds, bulbs, or cuttings for new flower

varieties. This financial tool ensures you have readily available resources to experiment with exciting new floral offerings.

- **Grants:** Explore government grants or agricultural development programs that incentivize using automated technologies in farming operations.
- **Vehicle Loans:** Consider financing options for acquiring essential equipment like delivery trucks or refrigerated vehicles. Efficient flower transportation is crucial for maintaining the quality and freshness of your blooms, and these loans will help you establish a robust delivery network that extends your reach to new customers.
- **Angel Investors:** If your diversification plans involve venturing into unique product offerings, consider connecting with angel investors. These individuals are often drawn to high-growth potential businesses and might be the perfect partners to help your innovative floral creations blossom.
- **Franchising Loans:** If your vision involves replicating your successful flower farm model through franchising, specific loan programs can support the initial costs associated with franchise development. These loans are the seeds that'll allow you to cultivate a network of flourishing flower farms, extending your brand's reach and impact.

Financial planning is the fertile ground from which successful expansion flourishes. Before diving into any funding option, conduct thorough research, compare rates and terms meticulously, and craft a comprehensive business plan. This plan should clearly outline your growth strategy, projected return on investment, and how the chosen funding will nurture your floral ambitions. Additionally, explore alternative financing avenues like crowdfunding platforms or forging partnerships with established companies in the floral industry.

# Establishing Satellite Farm Locations for Your Flower Business

Your flower farm is thriving, and the urge to expand beyond a single location might be tugging at your heartstrings. Establishing satellite farms offers significant benefits, such as increased production, diversified growing conditions, and access to new markets. However, venturing into multi-site operations requires careful planning and consideration. Here are the key aspects of establishing satellite farm locations:

**Managing Multiple Farm Sites:**

- **Centralized Management Systems:** Implement technology solutions like cloud-based software to ensure efficient communication, resource allocation, and data sharing across all farm locations.
- **Standardized Procedures:** Develop and implement standardized operating procedures (SOPs) for all aspects of your flower production process, ensuring consistency and quality across all your farms.

**Maintaining Brand Consistency:**

- **Develop a Brand Bible:** This document outlines your brand's core values, visual identity, and messaging, ensuring your brand personality shines through at every satellite location.
- **Regular Communication and Training:** Foster consistent communication and training programs for staff across all farms to uphold brand standards and customer service excellence.

**Navigating Legal Hurdles:**

- **Seek Legal Counsel:** Consult a lawyer specializing in agriculture and business expansion to ensure compliance with all necessary regulations, licensing requirements, and land-use laws specific to your chosen satellite locations.

- **Environmental Considerations:** Research and adhere to all environmental regulations concerning water usage, pesticide application, and waste disposal specific to each satellite location.

**Additional Considerations:**

- **Logistics and Transportation:** Plan to efficiently transport flowers, supplies, and personnel between your central farm and satellite locations.
- **Talent Acquisition and Management:** Develop a strategy to attract and retain skilled personnel for each satellite farm location, considering factors like local labor markets and potential relocation needs.

Establishing satellite farms is a complex yet rewarding endeavor. By carefully planning, implementing robust management systems, and navigating the legal landscape, you'll successfully expand your floral empire and cultivate success across multiple locations. Consider consulting with experienced agricultural professionals and seeking guidance from established multi-site flower businesses to learn and avoid potential pitfalls.

## Market Research and Expansion Strategies

Expansion is an exciting prospect, but venturing into new markets requires careful planning and strategic execution. Here are some tips on how to start your journey to successful floral expansion:

**Evaluating Risk and Contingencies:**

- **Market Research:** Conduct thorough market research to understand consumer preferences, price points, and potential competition in your target markets. Utilize resources like industry reports, surveys, and focus groups to gather valuable data and mitigate potential risks.
- **Develop Contingency Plans**: Be prepared for unforeseen circumstances by creating contingency

plans that address potential challenges like unexpected weather events, fluctuating flower prices, and logistical disruptions.

**Scaling Your Marketing Efforts:**

- **Tailored Marketing Strategies:** Tailor your marketing efforts to resonate with the specific demographics and choices of your target markets. It might involve adjusting your brand messaging, visual identity, and marketing channels to reach new audiences effectively.
- **Embrace Digital Marketing:** Leverage the power of digital marketing tools like social media advertising, search engine optimization (SEO), and influencer marketing to expand your brand reach and engage with potential customers in your target markets.

**Collaborative Partnerships and Alliances:**

- **Local Partnerships:** Partner with local businesses from within your target markets, such as event planners, florists, or wedding venues. These partnerships will provide valuable insights into local preferences and offer a springboard for establishing your brand presence.
- **Industry Collaborations:** Explore collaborative opportunities with other flower businesses, such as cooperative marketing initiatives or joint participation in trade shows. These collaborations will help you reach a wider audience and share resources for mutual benefit.

**Strategic Alliances with Distributors:**

- **Building Distributor Relationships:** Set up strong relationships with distributors in your target markets. Reliable distributors will ensure efficient logistics and delivery of your flowers, ensuring product freshness and customer satisfaction.

- **Negotiate Favorable Terms:** Negotiate favorable pricing and distribution terms with your chosen distributors to ensure your products remain competitive and profitable in your target markets.

**Continuous Improvement and Innovation:**

- **Data-driven Decision-making:** Leverage data insights from your marketing campaigns and sales performance to optimize your strategies and improve your approach to reaching new customers.
- **Embrace Innovation:** Stay at the forefront of the floral industry by taking on innovative practices like sustainable growing techniques, unique floral arrangements, and technology-driven solutions to increase efficiency.

Conduct thorough market research, implement well-defined marketing strategies, and foster strategic partnerships to confidently navigate the expansion process. Embrace continuous improvement and innovation, and watch your floral business blossom beyond all borders.

**Key Takeaways:**

- Self-assessment is key. Evaluate your farm's financial stability, operational efficiency, and market demand before expanding.
- Explore financing options. Consider various options like loans, grants, or partnerships to secure the necessary capital for growth initiatives.
- Satellite farms: weigh the pros and cons. Explore the possibilities and challenges of establishing additional farm locations to meet increased demand or diversify your offerings.
- Market research is your compass. Conduct thorough market research to identify potential new markets, understand customer preferences, and tailor your expansion strategy accordingly.

- Develop a comprehensive expansion plan. Draw up a detailed plan outlining your goals, timeline, budget, and marketing strategies for successful and sustainable growth.

By following these steps and embracing calculated growth, you'll be well on your way to transforming your flower farm from a local haven to a thriving floral enterprise. But the journey doesn't end here. In the next chapter, you'll explore the knowledge and strategies to navigate the inevitable hurdles that arise, ensuring your floral business blossoms through any storm.

# Chapter 7: Managing Challenges and Risks

"The best way out is always through," observed Robert Frost, aptly summarizing the spirit required to face challenges in any business endeavor. Flower farming is no exception and even the most meticulously planned operations encounter unexpected hurdles. This chapter equips you with the knowledge and strategies to identify potential risks, implement proactive measures, and navigate common challenges with resilience, ensuring your flower farm weathers any storm.

As you dive into this chapter, remember that even setbacks are valuable learning experiences. Embrace the opportunity to adapt, refine your approach, and emerge stronger from each challenge. By anticipating potential issues and proactively developing contingency plans, you'll be well-equipped to deal with the ups and downs of flower farming.

## Building a Fortress for Your Flower Business

The floral industry thrives on beauty and joy, but even the most vibrant flower bed faces potential challenges. As your flower business flourishes, identifying and mitigating potential risks ensures long-term success.

**Developing a Risk Management Plan:**

- **Proactive Approach:** Don't wait for disaster to strike. Instead, be proactive and identify potential risks and have a comprehensive risk management plan in place. This plan should outline strategies to mitigate, minimize, or transfer the impact of any potential threats.
- **Regular Review and Update:** Your risk management plan should be a living document. Regularly review and update it to reflect changes in

your business operations, the industry landscape, and the external environment.

**Weather-Related Challenges and Solutions:**

- **Understanding your Vulnerabilities:** Different areas face regional weather challenges. Understand your weather threats you are likely to face, such as excessive heat, drought, or freezing temperatures. The National Oceanic and Atmospheric Administration (NOAA) highlights the diverse weather patterns across the US, emphasizing the importance of location-specific risk assessment.
- **Implementing Mitigation Strategies:** Based on your study of weather risks, put plans in place to protect your crops. It might involve using greenhouse technology for temperature control, employing drought-resistant flower varieties, or investing in crop insurance as a financial safety net.

**Beyond the Basics:**

- **Market Fluctuations:** Explore potential risks associated with market fluctuations, such as changes in consumer preferences, flower shortages, or economic downturns. Develop strategies to diversify your offerings, build strong customer relationships, and maintain financial flexibility to weather market ups and downs.
- **Operational Disruptions:** Consider potential disruptions like equipment failures, labor shortages, or transportation delays. Implement preventative maintenance programs, build redundancy into your operations, and establish contingency plans to minimize the impact of these disruptions.

Even the most meticulous planning cannot eliminate all risks. However, by actively identifying potential threats and developing a comprehensive risk management plan, you'll equip your flower business with the resilience to weather any storm and ensure its continued bloom.

## Safeguarding Your Flower Farm from Pest and Disease Outbreaks

Your vibrant flower farm thrives on meticulous care and dedication. However, even the most meticulously nurtured blooms face the unseen threats of pest and disease outbreaks. These silent invaders have the potential to devastate your crops, leading to significant financial losses and emotional distress. Equipping yourself with the knowledge and implementing strategic measures will help you create a resilient floral haven that thrives under the shadow of potential threats.

### Integrated Pest Management (IPM)

This approach, championed by the United States Department of Agriculture (USDA), advocates for a holistic strategy prioritizing prevention over reactive measures. It involves:

- **Promoting a Healthy Ecosystem:** Attract beneficial insects and birds that naturally prey on harmful pests. Utilize techniques like planting companion plants or creating habitat areas to attract these natural allies.
- **Monitoring and Early Detection:** Regularly inspect your plants for signs of pests or diseases. Early detection allows swift intervention using biological controls like beneficial insects or organic pesticides derived from natural ingredients, minimizing reliance on harsh chemicals.
- **Cultural Practices:** Implement crop rotation, and proper sanitation, and manage growing conditions to discourage pests and pathogens.

### Investing in Knowledge and Monitoring

- **Stay Informed:** Regularly consult resources from the USDA, local agricultural extension services, and industry publications to stay updated on emerging pest and disease threats specific to your region and the flowers you cultivate.

- **Invest in Monitoring and Testing:** Regularly monitor your soil health and conduct routine testing for potential pests and diseases. Early detection means you can prevent any major problems from developing.
- **Embrace Continuous Learning:** Make sure you and your staff have the necessary knowledge to identify common pests and diseases. Educational programs offered by local agricultural organizations or online resources will be valuable tools.

**Mitigating Market Impact**

While proactive pest management is necessary, it's equally important to consider the potential economic impact of a pest or disease outbreak. Here's how you minimize market disruptions:

- **Diversify your Offerings:** Don't put all your eggs in one basket. By offering a diverse range of flower varieties, you'll mitigate the financial impact of a specific pest or disease affecting a particular type of flower.
- **Maintain Strong Customer Relationships:** Build customer trust and loyalty by consistently providing high-quality flowers and transparent communication. This goodwill will be a buffer during challenging times.

**Additional Considerations:**

- **Crop Insurance:** Explore crop insurance options to protect yourself from financial losses from crop failure due to pest or disease outbreaks.
- **Collaboration:** Collaborate with other local flower farms to share information and best practices regarding pest and disease management. This

collaborative approach builds a stronger community and allows for collective problem-solving.

Prevention is your weapon in the battle against pest and disease outbreaks. By implementing a comprehensive IPM program, investing in knowledge, and diversifying your offerings, you'll create a resilient flower farm that thrives and continues to bloom with success.

## Navigating Supply Chain Disruptions

The delicate bouquet of supply and demand in the flower industry is often disrupted by unforeseen challenges. From labor shortages to natural disasters, working through these disruptions requires resilience, adaptability, and strategic planning. Here are some common supply chain disruptions along with strategies to limit their impact:

**Labor Shortages and Recruitment:**

- **Competitive Compensation and Benefits:** In a competitive labor market, competitive wages, comprehensive benefits packages, and a positive work environment attract and retain skilled workers. Consider offering flexible work schedules, training opportunities, and career advancement pathways to enhance employee engagement.
- **Embrace Technology:** Explore labor-saving technologies like automated harvesting systems or irrigation controls to streamline processes and reduce reliance on manual labor. Automation has great potential in enhancing agricultural productivity and addressing labor shortages.

**Legal and Regulatory Challenges:**

- **Stay Informed:** Proactively stay updated on relevant legal and regulatory changes that might impact your flower farm's operations. It involves regulations concerning labor practices, environmental sustainability, or international trade. Utilize resources like industry associations, government websites, and legal consultations to stay compliant and avoid potential disruptions.

- **Build Relationships:** Strong relationships with regulatory agencies and industry organizations will help you to stay informed about any upcoming changes, seek guidance on compliance procedures, and potentially advocate for policies supporting the flower industry's sustainability and growth.

**Financial Setbacks and Recovery:**

- **Diversify your Customer Base:** Don't rely solely on a single customer or market segment. By diversifying your customer base, you spread the risk and minimize the impact of disruptions affecting specific channels. Explore new sales channels like online marketplaces, wholesale partnerships, or direct-to-consumer subscriptions.
- **Maintain a Healthy Financial Buffer:** Maintain a healthy financial buffer to weather unexpected financial setbacks caused by supply chain disruptions. It allows you to cover operational costs, invest in alternative solutions, and adapt to changing market conditions.

**Natural Disasters and Emergencies:**

- **Develop a Disaster Preparedness Plan:** Don't wait for disaster to strike. Develop a comprehensive disaster preparedness plan that outlines communication protocols, evacuation procedures, and business continuity strategies. This plan will minimize downtime, protect your workforce, and ensure a swift recovery.
- **Invest in Risk Mitigation Strategies:** Consider investing in risk mitigation strategies like crop insurance, flood barriers, or backup generators to protect your farm, equipment, and crops from potential damage caused by natural disasters.

**Insurance Coverage and Claims:**

- **Review your Insurance Coverage:** Regularly review your insurance coverage to ensure it protects your business against potential disruptions like weather events, transportation delays, or property damage. Consult with insurance professionals to identify any gaps and adjust your policies accordingly.
- **Filing Claims Efficiently:** In the event of a disruption, understand your insurance policy's claims process. Gather necessary documentation and file claims promptly to expedite the reimbursement process and minimize financial losses.

Supply chain disruptions are an unfortunate reality of the business world. Implementing these strategies will equip your flower farm with the resilience to navigate challenges, adapt to changing circumstances, and emerge stronger from any disruption. Be proactive, plan strategically, and embrace adaptability to ensure your floral enterprise continues to bloom, even in the face of unexpected storms.

## Crisis Communication Strategies for Your Flower Business

Even the most vibrant flower farms face occasional storms. While preventing every crisis might be impossible, navigating challenging situations effectively strengthens your brand and builds trust between your customers, staff, and suppliers. It's time to explore crucial crisis communication strategies to equip your flower business with resilience and clarity in the face of adversity:

**Evaluating and Learning from Failures:**

- **Conduct a Post-Crisis Review:** After a crisis, take time to analyze what went well and what could be improved in your communication response. This honest assessment, often facilitated by an external expert, helps identify areas for improvement and prevents repeating past mistakes.

- **Embrace Transparency and Continuous Learning:** Share your learnings from the crisis with your team publicly, demonstrating transparency and a commitment to learning and evolving. It fosters internal accountability and strengthens your commitment to open communication.

**Building Resilience in Your Business:**

- **Develop a Crisis Communication Plan:** Don't wait for a crisis to strike. Create a comprehensive plan outlining communication protocols, designated spokespersons, and key messages for various potential scenarios. This plan ensures a coordinated and efficient response when faced with unforeseen events.
- **Invest in Crisis Communication Training:** Train your team on crisis communication best practices. It empowers them to handle situations effectively, ensuring consistent messaging and clear communication across all channels.

**Scenario Planning and Preparedness:**

- **Identify Potential Threats:** Brainstorm and analyze potential crisis scenarios that could impact your business. This might involve issues like product recalls, weather disasters, or data breaches.
- **Develop Contingency Plans:** For each identified threat, create specific contingency plans outlining communication strategies, response protocols, and key decision-making processes. It reduces confusion and allows for swift action in a crisis.

**Developing a Risk Mitigation Culture:**

- **Proactive Communication:** Foster a culture of open communication within your organization.

Encourage employees to report potential issues early, allowing for proactive problem-solving and minimizing the risk of escalation.

- **Invest in Risk Management:** Implement robust risk management practices to identify and address potential threats before they evolve into full-blown crises.

Crisis communication is ultimately about building and maintaining trust. Prioritize open communication, learn from past experiences, and create a culture of preparedness. Navigate challenges with transparency and emerge stronger, building stronger relationships with your customers and stakeholders.

**Additional Tips:**

- **Emphasize Empathy and Understanding:** Acknowledge the concerns of those impacted by the crisis and demonstrate empathy in your communication.
- **Be Transparent and Truthful:** Avoid sugarcoating or manipulating the truth. Communicate openly and honestly, even when it's difficult.
- **Utilize Appropriate Channels:** Choose the communication channels best suited to reach your target audience. Consider social media, press releases, or direct communication depending on the situation and urgency.
- **Stay Consistent and Timely:** Keep your messaging consistent across all channels and provide timely updates throughout the crisis. It reduces confusion and fosters trust in your communication.

By adopting these strategies and cultivating a culture of open communication, your flower business will weather any storm and emerge even more vibrant and resilient.

## Blooming Through Challenges

While captivating in its beauty, the floral industry presents specific challenges for those cultivating and nurturing its success. From evolving consumer preferences to the pressures of competition, navigating this landscape requires resilience and self-care. Here are some common challenges faced by flower businesses and strategies to overcome them:

**Adapting to Shifting Consumer Preferences:**

- **Market Research:** Regularly conduct market research to understand evolving consumer preferences for flower varieties, arrangements, and sustainability practices. Utilize tools like surveys, focus groups, and social media analytics to stay ahead of the curve and adjust your products accordingly.
- **Innovation:** Explore innovative offers like locally sourced flowers, eco-friendly packaging, or subscription services to cater to the growing demand for sustainable and personalized floral experiences.

**Navigating Competition and Market Saturation:**

- **Differentiate your Brand:** Stand out from the crowd by developing a one-of-a-kind brand identity that reflects your values, aesthetic, and target audience. It involves focusing on specific flower types, offering unique arrangements, or building a strong local presence through community engagement.
- **Build Strategic Partnerships:** Collaborate with other businesses like event planners, designers, or local retailers to gain wider exposure and create value-added partnerships that benefit all parties involved.

**Managing Stress and Burnout:**

- **Prioritize Self-care:** The floral industry is physically and emotionally demanding. Prioritize self-care practices like regular exercise, healthy eating habits, and adequate sleep to manage stress and prevent burnout.
- **Build a Supportive Network:** Surround yourself with a supportive network of friends, family, and industry colleagues. Sharing your challenges and experiences with others will help you feel less alone.

**Emotional Well-being and Self-Care:**

- **Practice Mindfulness:** Techniques like meditation, deep breathing, and spending time in nature cultivate a sense of calm and help you manage stress levels.
- **Seek Professional Help:** Don't hesitate to seek professional help from therapists or counselors if you're struggling with stress, anxiety, or burnout. Prioritizing your mental well-being is essential for sustained success in any demanding profession.

**Time Management Strategies:**

- **Create a Schedule and Prioritize Tasks:** Develop a daily or weekly schedule that prioritizes essential tasks and allocates realistic timeframes for their completion. Utilize tools like calendars, planners, and to-do lists to stay organized and avoid feeling overwhelmed.
- **Delegate and Automate Tasks:** When possible, delegate tasks to colleagues or leverage technology to automate repetitive processes. It frees up valuable time for you to focus on strategic planning, customer interaction, and creative pursuits.

Challenges are an inherent part of any business journey. Understand the specific challenges of the flower industry, equip yourself with coping mechanisms, and embrace a growth mindset. Navigating these hurdles with resilience will cultivate a thriving floral haven.

**Key Takeaways:**

- Proactive identification of risks. Familiarize yourself with potential risks like pest outbreaks, weather events, supply chain disruptions, and market fluctuations.
- Develop contingency plans. Create detailed plans outlining how you will respond to various challenges, ensuring quick and effective action during difficult times.
- Mastering crisis communication. Develop clear and concise communication strategies to effectively address concerns and maintain trust with customers and partners during challenging situations.
- Navigating industry-specific challenges. Understand and prepare for common industry issues like labor shortages, competition, and fluctuations in flower prices.
- Embrace continuous learning. Stay informed about industry trends, emerging threats, and best practices for risk mitigation through ongoing learning and professional development.

By cultivating a proactive mindset and implementing the strategies outlined in this chapter, you'll be well-equipped to navigate the inevitable challenges that arise in flower farming. Building strong relationships with your customers will pave the way for sustained success as you move forward. In the next chapter, you'll uncover strategies for rewarding loyalty and creating lifelong flower enthusiasts of your customers. So, turn the page and get started with building lasting customer connections.

# Chapter 8: Customer Relationship Management

**"The best way to predict your future is to create it." - Abraham Lincoln**

As your flower farm flourishes, the success of your business becomes inextricably linked to the satisfaction and loyalty of your customers. This chapter explores the art of customer relationship management (CRM), equipping you with the strategies and tools to build meaningful connections, nurture loyalty, and ensure your customers return time and again for your floral creations.

## Building and Maintaining Customer Loyalty

Flower farming is where beauty and emotions intertwine. Strong customer relationships are the lifeblood of your business. These relationships go beyond a single sale. They're about creating a lasting connection that keeps customers coming back for more. Prepare to explore some proven strategies for building and maintaining flourishing customer relationships:

**Effective Communication with Customers:**

- **Multiple Communication Channels:** Don't limit yourself to one channel. Utilize a mix of email marketing, social media engagement, and personalized text messages to stay connected with your customers and share updates, promotions, and special offers.
- **Transparency and Clarity:** Be transparent in your communication, clearly outlining product information, delivery policies, and return procedures. It builds trust and fosters a positive customer experience.

**Personalized Customer Service:**

- **Note their Preferences:** Go the extra mile by remembering customer preferences like favorite flowers, anniversaries, or special occasions. This personalized touch creates a memorable experience and strengthens the connection.
- **Actively Listen:** Take the time to actively listen to your customers' needs and preferences. You'll be able to tailor your recommendations, address their concerns, and deliver a service that exceeds expectations.

**Handling Customer Inquiries and Complaints:**

- **Prompt Response Times:** Respond to customer inquiries and complaints promptly and professionally. Even if you don't have an immediate answer, acknowledge their message and let them know you're working on a solution. Timely responses are paramount in managing customer sentiment.
- **Empathy and Problem-solving:** Approach customer concerns with empathy and a genuine desire to resolve the issue. Offer fair, efficient solutions, and leave the customer feeling heard and valued.

**Addressing Customer Feedback:**

- **Collect Feedback Actively:** Don't wait for feedback to come to you. Proactively seek customer feedback through post-purchase surveys, online reviews, or social media polls. It allows you to identify areas for improvement and demonstrate your commitment to customer satisfaction.
- **Respond Publicly to Positive and Negative Feedback:** Acknowledge and thank customers for positive feedback, showing appreciation for their loyalty. For negative feedback, respond publicly, apologize for any shortcomings, and outline the steps you're taking to address the issue. It

demonstrates transparency and a commitment to continuous improvement.

Building strong customer relationships is an ongoing process. Consistently implement these strategies to nurture lasting connections with your customers, turning them from one-time buyers into loyal brand advocates who keep your floral business blooming.

## How a CRM System Cultivates Customer Loyalty

In the competitive floral industry, building strong customer relationships is the lifeblood of your business. However, as your customer base grows, keeping track of individual preferences and tailoring your approach feels like trying to manage a sprawling, diverse garden. The Customer Relationship Management (CRM) system is a powerful tool that helps you nurture flourishing customer relationships and cultivate a loyal customer base, boosting your bottom line in the process.

**Leverage Customer Insights for Targeted Engagement:**

- **Understand your Audience:** A robust CRM system goes beyond simply storing customer contact information. It allows you to segment your customers based on factors like purchase history, demographics, and occasion preferences. This in-depth understanding helps you paint a clearer picture of who your customers are, what they like, and how they interact with your business.
- **Tailored Marketing and Communication:** Knowing your customer segments intimately allows you to move beyond generic marketing tactics and craft targeted messages and communication strategies that resonate with their specific needs and preferences. Send personalized birthday greetings with exclusive discount codes to high-value customers or offer seasonal flower arrangement

recommendations to those who frequently purchase for special occasions. This level of personalization will dramatically increase engagement rates, conversion rates, and overall customer satisfaction.

**Implement Customer Retention Strategies:**

- **Identify your Champions:** Your CRM helps you identify your most loyal customers, the ones who consistently contribute significantly to your revenue and brand advocacy. You can then focus your retention efforts on these valuable customers, ensuring they feel appreciated and valued.
- **Personalized Engagement:** Utilize your CRM data to personalize your communication and offers for loyal customers. Send birthday wishes, special occasion reminders, and exclusive promotions to show appreciation and encourage repeat business. You can even offer them exclusive previews to new products or loyalty program benefits to further solidify their connection with your brand.

**Create a Rewarding Loyalty Program:**

- **Effortless Program Management:** A CRM streamlines the loyalty program's creation and management, turning what could be a cumbersome task into a smooth and efficient process. Track customer points, reward purchases, and manage redemption processes, all within the centralized CRM platform. It frees up your time and resources to focus on delivering exceptional customer service and growing your business.
- **Boost Customer Engagement and Loyalty:** A well-designed loyalty program, powered by your CRM incentivizes repeat purchases and strengthens customer relationships in a way that generic marketing tactics often cannot. By rewarding loyal customers for their continued support, you create an environment that appreciates brand loyalty and

encourages them to choose your flower shop over your competitors, even when faced with enticing alternatives.

**Unlock the Power of Customer Data:**

- **Gather Valuable Insights:** Your CRM becomes more than just a contact list. It transforms into a central repository for customer data, including purchase history, communication preferences, and feedback. Analyze this data to understand your customers' behavior and preferences. Understand what types of flowers are popular, and what occasions drive the most sales, and even identify potential of cross-selling opportunities.
- **Data-driven Decision-making:** Use the information from your customer data to make informed decisions about every aspect of your business. Optimize your product offerings by stocking popular flower varieties and catering to specific customer segments. Refine your marketing campaigns to target the right audience with the right message at the right time. Ultimately, data-driven decision-making powered by your CRM allows you to make strategic choices that drive business growth and customer satisfaction.

**Proactively Gather Feedback and Improve:**

- **Seamless Feedback Collection:** Integrate customer satisfaction surveys directly into your CRM system. It allows you to collect real-time feedback after purchases or interactions with your brand, giving you priceless knowledge about the areas where you're exceeding expectations and those where you can improve.
- **Turn Feedback into Action:** Respond promptly to negative feedback and address customer concerns efficiently. It shows your commitment to customer satisfaction and can turn a disgruntled customer

into a loyal one. Additionally, analyze positive and negative feedback to identify recurring themes and implement improvements that enhance the overall customer experience.

**Utilize Upselling and Cross-selling Techniques Strategically:**

- **Identify Relevant Recommendations:** Utilize your CRM data to identify relevant product recommendations for individual customers. By understanding their purchase history and preferences, you can suggest complementary flower arrangements, vases, gift baskets, or other relevant products that enhance their experience and potentially increase their order value.
- **Increase Revenue Potential:** Strategically recommending relevant products based on customer data creates a win-win situation. Customers discover products they might genuinely enjoy, and your business benefits from increased average order value and a boost in overall revenue. The key is to make genuine recommendations, not pushy sales.

A CRM system is not a magic solution but a powerful tool. To truly cultivate flourishing customer relationships, combine the power of data with genuine care and personalized communication. By implementing these strategies and building meaningful connections with your customers, your flower business will blossom into a thriving success story, one satisfied customer at a time.

## Referral Programs and Incentives

Referral programs and incentives offer a powerful way to cultivate loyalty, not just by acknowledging your existing customers, but by encouraging them to become brand ambassadors and spread the love (and blooms) further. Here are some strategies to make your flower business blossom:

**Celebrating Customer Milestones:**

- **Birthdays and Anniversaries:** Leverage your CRM system to identify customer birthdays and anniversaries. Send personalized greetings with exclusive discounts or special offers, showing you value their business and care about their celebrations.
- **Purchase Milestones:** Celebrate customer milestones like reaching a specific purchase threshold or becoming a repeat customer. Offer them personalized rewards, early access to new products, or exclusive discounts. The effectiveness of loyalty programs in driving repeat business is unparalleled, with most customers likely to continue shopping at a store with a program in which they participate.

**Social Media Engagement with Customers:**

- **Run Competitions and Giveaways:** Host engaging competitions and giveaways on social media platforms, encouraging customers to share their experiences with your brand and tag their friends. It increases brand awareness, incentivizes referrals, and encourages a community spirit around your flower business.
- **Feature Customer Stories:** Showcase customer testimonials and positive reviews on your social media pages. It builds trust and credibility, encouraging potential customers to choose your business and inspiring existing customers to continue spreading the word.

**Responding to Online Reviews:**

- **Engage with Positive Reviews:** Acknowledge and express gratitude for positive reviews. It shows you value customer feedback and appreciate their loyalty.

- **Address Negative Reviews Professionally:** Respond promptly and professionally to negative reviews. Offer solutions to any problems and demonstrate your commitment to customer satisfaction. This proactive approach turns a disgruntled customer into a satisfied one, potentially encouraging them to return and leave a revised review, further enhancing your brand reputation.

**Email Marketing for Customer Engagement:**

- **Targeted Email Campaigns:** Segment your customer base and send targeted email campaigns with personalized offers and promotions relevant to their interests and purchase history. It increases engagement and encourages them to share your emails with friends and family who might be interested in your products.
- **Referral Program Emails:** Promote your referral program through engaging email campaigns. Clearly outline the benefits of participating, highlight the rewards offered for successful referrals, and provide easy-to-use referral links to share with friends and family.

**Customer Appreciation Events:**

- **Host Exclusive Events:** Organize exclusive events for your most loyal customers, offering them early access to new products, workshops with floral arrangement tutorials, or special discounts. It demonstrates your appreciation for their continued support and encourages a sense of community and belonging.
- **Partner with Local Businesses:** Collaborate with businesses in complementary industries, like bakeries or cafes, to host joint events offering special packages or discounts. It expands your reach, attracts new customers who might be

interested in both businesses and strengthens existing customer relationships through unique and memorable experiences.

Creating a successful referral program goes beyond simply offering incentives. Celebrate customer milestones, engage with them on social media, address their concerns, and express genuine appreciation. Aim to foster a sense of connection and loyalty beyond the transactional. By implementing these strategies and making your customers feel valued and appreciated, you cultivate a thriving community of brand advocates, ensuring your flower business blooms long into the future.

## Providing Value-Added Services to Cultivate Customer Loyalty

In the floral industry, offering stunning blooms is just the beginning. To truly stand out in a competitive landscape, businesses need to go beyond the bouquet and provide value-added services that cultivate customer loyalty and position you as a trusted advisor in the floral experience. It's time to explore some strategies that add value and nurture lasting customer relationships:

**Empowering Customers through Education and Resources:**

- **Flower Care Guides:** Offer comprehensive flower care guides on your website or social media platforms. Provide tips on proper handling, storage, and vase life extension. It empowers your customers and ensures their flowers remain fresh and beautiful for longer, improving their overall satisfaction.
- **Floral Arrangement Tutorials:** Host online or in-person workshops on flower arranging. It gives customers valuable skills and builds a sense of community and engagement with your brand.

**Cultivating Long-Term Relationships:**

- **Go Beyond the Initial Purchase:** Understand that customer value extends beyond a single transaction. Implement a system to track customer lifetime value (CLV), considering factors like purchase history, frequency, and average order value. Identify your most valuable customers and tailor your marketing and loyalty programs accordingly.
- **Invest in Customer Retention:** By focusing on retaining existing customers, you tap into a more reliable source of revenue compared to the often costly process of acquiring new ones. An increase in customer retention will boost your profits significantly.

**Building a Thriving Brand Community:**

- **Create a Dedicated Online Space:** Create a sense of community by a dedicated online space, like a private Facebook group or forum, where customers can connect, share experiences, and learn from each other. It creates a sense of belonging and strengthens their connection to your brand.
- **Host Online and Offline Events:** Organize events that go beyond flower sales. Host floral design workshops, partner with local businesses for joint events, or offer virtual consultations with floral experts. These experiences create lasting memories and strengthen customer loyalty.

**Recognizing and Rewarding Loyal Customers:**

- **Loyalty Programs:** Implement a well-structured loyalty program that rewards customers for their continued support. Offer tiered rewards based on purchase history, provide exclusive discounts or exclusive previews to new products, and celebrate milestones with personalized greetings and offers.
- **Personalized Recognition:** Go beyond generic rewards. Show your appreciation for individual

customers by acknowledging their birthdays or anniversaries, noting their preferences, and offering them personalized recommendations or discounts based on their past purchases.

**Handling Difficult Customer Situations:**

- **Active Listening and Empathy:** When faced with a difficult customer, prioritize active listening and empathy. Acknowledge their concerns, apologize for any inconvenience caused, and work towards a solution that addresses their needs fairly and efficiently.
- **Proactive Communication:** Keep your customers informed throughout the process of resolving an issue. Provide timely updates and follow through on your commitments. It demonstrates transparency and builds trust, even in challenging situations.

Providing value-added services is not just about offering additional features. It's about creating a holistic and enriching experience for your customers. Empower them with knowledge, build a community, and demonstrate genuine appreciation to cultivate loyal brand advocates who are happy to return for your beautiful blooms and eager to spread the word and keep your floral business booming.

**Key Takeaways:**

- Prioritize personalized service. Take the time to understand your customers' needs and preferences, personalize your interactions, and create a memorable experience.
- Embrace CRM technology. Consider implementing a customer relationship management (CRM) system to streamline communication, track interactions, and personalize your outreach.

- Incentivize referrals. Encourage customer referrals and loyalty through creative programs and rewards, fostering a sense of community and expanding your reach.
- Add value beyond flowers. Explore offering additional services like flower arranging workshops, subscription boxes, or special occasion delivery options to engage your customers further and add value to their experience.
- Seek feedback and adapt. Actively ask for feedback through surveys, reviews, or direct conversations, and use it to refine your offerings and continuously improve your customer service.

By implementing these strategies and making genuine connections with your customers, you'll cultivate a loyal following that celebrates your floral artistry and contributes to the long-term success of your flower farm. As technology continues to evolve, the possibilities for innovation and growth are limitless. In the following chapter on technology and innovation, you'll explore exciting ways to leverage technology to streamline operations, enhance customer experiences, and stay ahead of the curve in the ever-evolving world of flower farming.

# Chapter 9: Technology and Innovation

"The future belongs to those who believe in the beauty of their dreams," Eleanor Roosevelt envisioned a future driven by innovation and the pursuit of progress.

As the flower farming industry evolves, embracing technological advancements becomes increasingly essential to optimize efficiency, enhance customer experience, and maintain a competitive edge. This chapter explores technology's exciting possibilities, empowering you to integrate innovative solutions into your farm and propel your floral dreams toward a flourishing future.

## How Technology is Revolutionizing Agriculture

The image of farming often evokes rustic scenes of tractors and sun-baked fields. However, the reality of modern agriculture is increasingly intertwined with the world of technology. From sophisticated software to state-of-the-art sensors, a wave of innovation is transforming how people grow food, making it more efficient, sustainable, and profitable. Here are some key technologies shaping the future of farming:

**Farm Management Software:**

- **Streamlining Operations:** Ditch the spreadsheets and fragmented data management. Farm management software offers a central hub to track everything from planting schedules and yield data to inventory management and financial records. It allows you to streamline operations, improve decision-making, and gain valuable insights into your farm's performance.
- **Precision is Key:** Many software solutions integrate with other farm technologies like weather stations and soil sensors. It allows for data-driven decision-making, enabling you to optimize resource

use, such as water and fertilizer, based on real-time data and historical trends.

**Weather and Climate Prediction Tools:**

- **Mitigating Risk:** Mother Nature is unpredictable, but advanced weather and climate prediction tools will help you prepare. These tools provide detailed forecasts, including temperature, precipitation, and even pest outbreak risks, allowing you to make informed decisions about planting schedules, irrigation plans, and potential pest control measures.
- **Adapting to Change:** Climate change is a growing concern for farmers. Advanced tools will help you adapt by providing long-term climate projections and identifying potential challenges like increased drought or flooding risks. It'll allow you to adopt suitable crop varieties and implement proactive water management strategies.

**Soil Testing and Analysis Technology:**

- **Understanding Your Land:** Soil is the foundation of a healthy farm. Advanced soil testing and analysis technologies provide detailed insights into nutrient levels, microbial activity, and even soil structure. It empowers you to make informed decisions about fertilizer application, ensuring optimal nutrient delivery to your crops and minimizing environmental impact.
- **Precision Fertilization:** By understanding the specific needs of the soil, you can be precise and economical when adopting fertilization practices. It means applying the right type and amount of fertilizer in the right place at the right time. It improves crop yields, reduces fertilizer waste, and protects water quality.

**Crop Monitoring and Data Collection:**

- **Keeping a Close Eye:** High-resolution drone cameras with specialized sensors are revolutionizing crop monitoring. These aerial platforms capture detailed images of fields, allowing you to identify issues like disease outbreaks, nutrient deficiencies, or irrigation problems early on.
- **Data-Driven Decisions:** The data collected through various technologies can be analyzed using sophisticated software, generating insights into crop health, growth patterns, and potential yield. It empowers you to make informed decisions about resource allocation, pest control strategies, and harvesting schedules.

Incorporating technology into farming is not a one-size-fits-all solution. The specific technologies will depend on each farm's size, location, and specific needs. However, by embracing innovation, you'll unlock a world of possibilities, optimize your operations, and ensure a more sustainable and productive future for agriculture.

## Cultivating Efficiency

In today's agricultural landscape, efficiency is critical. Every drop of water, every minute spent, and every dollar invested needs to be optimized for maximum yield and profitability. This is where automated irrigation systems come into play, acting as a powerful tool for streamlining your farm operations, saving resources, and boosting your bottom line. It's time to explore how automation extends beyond watering:

**Greenhouse Automation and Control:**

- **Precise Climate Management:** Automated systems can precisely manage temperature, humidity, and even ventilation within greenhouses. It creates an ideal growing environment for your crops, leading to improved yield, reduced disease risk, and optimized resource use.

- **Remote Monitoring and Control:** Many systems offer remote access through mobile apps or web interfaces, allowing you to monitor and adjust greenhouse conditions from anywhere, anytime. It provides greater flexibility and control over your crops, even when you're not physically present at the farm.

**Inventory and Supply Chain Management:**

- **Real-time Tracking and Visibility:** Automated systems can track inventory levels of seeds, fertilizers, and other supplies in real time. It eliminates the need for manual inventory checks and ensures you have the necessary resources readily available, minimizing delays and disruptions in your operations.
- **Data-Driven Decision Making:** By analyzing inventory data, you gain valuable insights into your resource usage patterns and predict future needs. It allows you to optimize ordering and purchasing practices, reducing waste and minimizing unnecessary costs.

**Online Sales and E-commerce Platforms:**

- **Direct-to-Consumer Marketing:** Automate your sales process by setting up an online store or integrating with existing e-commerce platforms. It allows you to sell your produce directly to consumers, eliminating middlemen and potentially increasing your profit margins.
- **Convenient Customer Experience:** Automated ordering systems provide a convenient way for customers to purchase your products online. It includes features like secure payment gateways, real-time order tracking, and automated order confirmation emails.

**Social Media Marketing Tools:**

- **Reach a Wider Audience:** Utilize social media scheduling tools to automate publishing engaging content showcasing your farm, your produce, and your commitment to sustainable practices. It helps you build brand awareness, connect with potential customers, and promote your offerings.
- **Targeted Audience Engagement:** Utilize social media analytics tools to understand your audience's demographics and interests. It allows you to tailor your social media content to resonate with specific segments of your audience, increasing engagement and driving sales.

**Email Marketing Software:**

- **Automated Campaigns and Newsletters:** Use email marketing software to automate sending targeted campaigns and newsletters to your customer base. It allows you to share updates about your farm, promote new products, and offer special deals, all while nurturing customer relationships.
- **Track and Analyze Engagement:** Monitor the performance of your email campaigns to see what resonates with your audience. This data allows you to refine your approach and ensure your email marketing efforts effectively reach and engage your customers.

**Financial Management Software:**

- **Automated Accounting and Recordkeeping:** To simplify your life, embrace automated financial management software. It'll track your income, expenses, and profitability, providing valuable insights into your farm's financial health.
- **Streamlined Reporting and Analysis:** Generate automated reports and financial statements easily. It simplifies tax filing, helps identify areas for cost savings, and empowers you to make informed financial decisions for your farm.

**Customer Relationship Management (CRM):**

- **Centralized Customer Data:** Use a CRM system to store and manage customer information, including purchase history, preferences, and communication history. It allows you to personalize your interactions with each customer, build stronger relationships, and foster loyalty.
- **Automated Communication and Follow-up:** Automate personalized communication with your customers, sending birthday greetings, order confirmation emails, or special offer notifications. It strengthens customer relationships and increases the likelihood of repeat business.

**Mobile Apps for Farm Management:**

- **On-the-go Monitoring and Control:** Access your farm data, control irrigation systems, and manage various aspects of your operation from anywhere with a mobile app. It provides greater flexibility and allows you to stay connected to your farm even when you're on the go.

Automation is just one tool in your agricultural toolbox. Choose the right systems and integrate them effectively with your existing practices. Embracing automation strategically will streamline your operations, optimize resource use, and cultivate a thriving farm for years.

## Exploring Drones and Aerial Imaging in Flower Farming

From delicate roses to vibrant sunflowers, flower farms cultivate beauty and bring joy to countless occasions. However, beneath the picturesque surface lies a complex industry that is constantly adapting and innovating. Drones and aerial imaging are revolutionizing how flower farmers manage their fields, optimize yields, and navigate the industry's evolving landscape.

**Biotechnology in Flower Farming:**

- **Disease and Pest Resistance:** Scientists are developing genetically modified flowers with enhanced resistance to diseases and pests, potentially reducing reliance on chemical pesticides and promoting sustainable practices. However, ethical considerations and consumer concerns regarding GMOs remain a significant discussion point.
- **Improved Flower Characteristics:** Research is exploring the possibility of using genetic modification to create flowers with longer shelf life, stronger stems, or more vibrant colors. While this holds potential benefits for growers and consumers, the long-term ecological and societal implications of such modifications need careful evaluation.

**Sustainability Technology Solutions:**

- **Precision Irrigation:** Drones equipped with multispectral sensors can map water needs across a field, allowing for targeted irrigation and minimizing water waste. It conserves resources and reduces the environmental impact of flower farming.
- **Soil Analysis:** By analyzing aerial imagery, you gain insights into soil health and nutrient distribution. This data-driven approach allows for informed decisions about fertilizer application, minimizing environmental pollution, and optimizing resource use.

**Research and Development Initiatives:**

- **Pollinator Health:** Drones equipped with special cameras can be used to monitor pollinator populations within fields. This data informs strategies to protect these vital insects, whose health is crucial for flower production and overall ecosystem balance.

- **Early Disease Detection:** Drones equipped with thermal cameras can detect subtle changes in plant temperature, potentially identifying diseases at an early stage. It allows for prompt intervention and minimizes crop loss, ultimately benefiting both farmers and consumers.

**Industry Innovations and Trends:**

- **Autonomous Crop Monitoring:** Advances in artificial intelligence are paving the way for autonomous drone flights for routine field monitoring. It frees up valuable time for farmers and allows for more frequent data collection, leading to improved decision-making and crop management.
- **Vertical Farming:** Drones are being used for monitoring and data collection in vertical farming facilities, which are becoming increasingly popular due to their space-efficient and environmentally controlled environments.

The use of drones and aerial imaging in flower farming is not without its challenges. Privacy concerns, regulations surrounding airspace usage, and the cost of using these technologies are all factors to consider. However, the potential benefits are undeniable. As research and development continue, drones are poised to take flight as a powerful tool for flower farmers, leading to a future where beauty and innovation bloom together.

## Budgeting, Training, and Security for Businesses Embracing Technology

Technology is no longer an option, it's a necessity in the current market. Navigating the tech world is daunting, especially regarding budgeting, training, and ensuring data security. It's time to dive into these crucial aspects to make informed decisions and ensure a smooth technological journey for your business:

**Technology Budgeting and ROI Analysis:**

- **Align with Business Goals:** Before diving into the latest gadgets, clearly define your business goals. What problems are you trying to solve, or what opportunities are you trying to capture, with technology? This roadmap ensures you invest in solutions that directly contribute to your overall business objectives.
- **Cost-benefit Analysis:** Don't just get swept up in the excitement of new technology. Conduct a thorough cost-benefit analysis for each potential investment. Consider the initial purchase price, ongoing maintenance costs, potential training, and the expected return on investment (ROI). Consider factors like increased efficiency, improved customer satisfaction, or a competitive edge.

**Training and Skill Development:**

- **Upskilling your Workforce:** Technology is only as effective as the people who use it. Invest in training programs to equip your employees with the necessary skills to utilize new technologies effectively. It maximizes the return on your technology investment and generates a culture of continuous learning and adaptability within your organization.
- **Microlearning and On-demand Resources:** Consider implementing microlearning strategies, offering bite-sized training modules that are easily accessible and can be completed at the employee's convenience. Additionally, explore on-demand resources like online tutorials or knowledge bases for readily available information and troubleshooting assistance.

**Collaborating with Tech Providers:**

- **Seek Partnerships, not just Vendors:** Look beyond simply purchasing technology from a provider. Build strategic partnerships with tech companies who understand your business needs and offer ongoing support, guidance, and potential customization options. This collaborative approach will be a long-term relationship and ensures you get the most out of your technology investments.

- **Clear Communication and Expectations:** When working with any tech provider, maintain clear communication and establish realistic expectations from the outset. Clearly outline your needs, goals, and timelines, and ensure the provider understands your specific requirements. It prevents misunderstandings and ensures a smooth implementation process.

**Data Security and Privacy:**

- **Prioritize Data Protection:** Data security and privacy are paramount. Robust cybersecurity measures to safeguard your company's sensitive information and protect your customers' data are essential. It includes regularly updating software, employing strong password protocols, and conducting employee training on cybersecurity best practices.
- **Stay Informed and Compliant:** The regulatory landscape surrounding data privacy is constantly evolving. Stay informed about relevant regulations and ensure your business practices comply with them. It minimizes the risk of legal repercussions and builds trust and transparency with your customers.

Embracing technology is a continuous journey. Carefully plan your budget, invest in training, collaborate effectively with tech providers, and prioritize data security. You'll then confidently navigate the ever-changing tech landscape, empowering your business to thrive in the digital age.

**Key Takeaways:**

- Explore automated irrigation systems. Implement technology-driven irrigation solutions to conserve water, optimize resource usage, and ensure consistent moisture levels for your crops.
- Harness the power of drones and aerial imaging. Utilize drones for aerial photography and crop monitoring, plant health, growth patterns, and potential risk issues.
- Stay informed about research and development. Keep yourself updated on emerging technologies and research initiatives in the flower farming industry, identifying opportunities to incorporate advancements into your farm.
- Budgeting and ROI analysis. Allocate resources strategically for technological advancements, conducting thorough cost-benefit analyses to ensure a positive return on investment (ROI).
- Embrace continuous learning. Remain open to learning new technologies and adapting your approach as the digital landscape of flower farming continues to evolve.

Adapting to new technologies requires careful consideration, planning, and a willingness to learn. Embrace the growth potential, conduct thorough research, and seek guidance from experts when needed to ensure you leverage technology effectively for the sustainable success of your farm.

As your business expands and flourishes, navigating legal and regulatory compliance becomes crucial. In Chapter 10: Legal and Regulatory Compliance, you'll discover the essential legal considerations, licensing requirements, and best practices to ensure your farm operates within the framework of the law and fosters a sustainable and ethical business environment.

# Chapter 10: Legal and Regulatory Compliance

"Ignorance of the law excuses no one," wrote legal scholar William Blackstone, highlighting the importance of understanding the legal and regulatory framework within which any business operates. As your flower farm blossoms, navigating the intricacies of legalities becomes paramount. This chapter will equip you with the foundational knowledge of relevant regulations, ensuring your business operates ethically, sustainably, and fully complies with the law.

As you go into the legal aspects of your flower farm, seeking professional guidance from legal and agricultural experts is highly recommended. This chapter gives you an overview, but navigating specific regulations is complex and nuanced. Consulting professionals will safeguard your business and ensure peace of mind.

## Understanding Local Agricultural Regulations

Turning your passion for agriculture into a thriving business is an exciting endeavor. However, navigating the often complex world of regulations feels overwhelming. It's time to break down essential local agricultural regulations to help you navigate the legal landscape and ensure your farm operates smoothly:

**Zoning and Land Use Regulations:**

- **Understanding Zoning Restrictions:** Different zones within a county or municipality have specific land-use regulations. Familiarize yourself with your property's zoning designation and any restrictions on agricultural activities, livestock, or structures. Websites of local planning departments often provide zoning maps and regulations.

**Environmental Permits and Approvals:**

- **Water Management Considerations:** Depending on the size and nature of your farm, you might need permits for water use, irrigation, or potential discharges. Contact your local environmental protection agency or department of agriculture for guidance on obtaining necessary permits and ensuring your practices comply with environmental regulations.
- **Air Quality and Waste Disposal:** Regulations may exist regarding air emissions from farm activities like burning or specific waste disposal practices. Consulting with your local environmental agency will ensure you comply with regulations and operate sustainably.

**Business Licenses and Permits:**

- **State and Local Business Licenses:** Most localities require businesses, including farms, to obtain a business license to operate legally. Research the specific licenses required in your area and contact your local government office for details on the application process and any fees involved.
- **Specialty Permits:** You might need additional permits depending on your specific agricultural activities. For example, raising livestock might require a permit from the Department of Agriculture or Animal Control. Do your research and get any permits necessary to avoid legal repercussions and ensure responsible operation.

**Agricultural Tax Considerations:**

- **Tax Breaks and Incentives:** Explore potential tax breaks and incentives available to agricultural businesses in your area. It includes property tax breaks, income tax deductions, or exemptions for specific agricultural equipment. Consulting a tax professional or contacting your local agricultural extension office will help you navigate these benefits effectively.

- **Record-keeping:** Maintain accurate records of your farm's income and expenses. It simplifies tax filing and provides valuable data for informed business decisions and potential discussions with lenders or government agencies.

**Employment and Labor Laws:**

- **Understanding labor laws:** If you employ workers on your farm, familiarize yourself with federal and state labor laws regarding minimum wage, overtime pay, child labor restrictions, and workplace safety regulations. The US Department of Labor provides comprehensive resources and guidance on its website.

## Building a Secure Workplace

Ensuring the safety and well-being of your employees is not only an ethical responsibility but also a legal requirement. Regardless of size or industry, businesses must navigate a complex web of legal regulations to create a safe and compliant work environment. Here are the key areas of legal focus to protect your employees and your business:

**Product Labeling and Packaging Requirements:**

- **Accurate and Clear Information:** Ensure your products are labeled accurately and comply with relevant federal regulations. It includes information on ingredients, potential hazards, usage instructions, and safety warnings. The Consumer Product Safety Commission (CPSC) provides comprehensive guidelines for various product categories.
- **Mitigating Risk and Liability:** Clear and compliant product labeling minimizes the risk of

accidents, injuries, and potential lawsuits claiming negligence.

**Intellectual Property Rights:**

- **Protecting your Innovations:** If your business has developed products, inventions, or even branding elements, consider securing intellectual property (IP) protection through patents, trademarks, or copyrights. It safeguards your ownership and prevents unauthorized use by competitors.
- **Seeking Legal Advice:** Consulting with an intellectual property attorney can help you navigate the intricacies of IP protection, ensuring your valuable assets are adequately protected.

**Contracts and Agreements:**

- **Formalizing Agreements:** Clearly defined contracts with vendors, suppliers, and even employees are essential for establishing expectations, outlining responsibilities, and minimizing the risk of misunderstandings or disputes.
- **Clear Communication and Record-keeping:** Ensure all contracts are written, reviewed by both parties and properly signed and documented. It provides a paper trail in case of any future disagreements.

**Insurance Coverage and Liability:**

- **Assessing your Needs:** Obtain appropriate liability insurance to protect your business from financial repercussions in case of accidents, injuries, or lawsuits. It includes general liability insurance, workers' compensation insurance, and other relevant coverage depending on your industry and operations.

- **Risk Mitigation and Peace of Mind:** Adequate insurance coverage provides a safety net, minimizing potential financial losses and allowing you to focus on running your business with peace of mind.

**Trademarks and Branding Protection:**

- **Safeguarding your Brand Identity:** Your brand name, logo, and other unique branding elements are valuable assets. Registering your trademarks with the United States Patent and Trademark Office (USPTO) protects them from unauthorized use by competitors.
- **Building Brand Trust:** A strong and legally protected brand identity fosters trust with customers and creates a competitive advantage in the marketplace.

**Handling Legal Disputes and Claims:**

- **Early Intervention and Communication:** In the unfortunate event of a legal dispute or claim, prioritize early intervention. Address concerns promptly and maintain open communication with all parties involved.
- **Seeking Legal Counsel:** Consulting with a qualified lawyer is crucial when navigating legal matters. They will advise you on your rights and options, represent you in court if necessary, and advocate for your best interests.

Legal compliance is a continuous process. Staying informed about relevant regulations, seeking professional guidance when needed, and prioritizing safety within your workplace are essential steps in protecting your employees, your business, and its future success.

## Cultivating Trust with Organic Compliance

Consumers are increasingly seeking organic products, driven by a desire for healthy, sustainable, and ethically sourced food and other products. To meet this demand and build trust with your customers, ensure you comply with organic standards. Here are the primary aspects of organic compliance, empowering you to navigate the regulations and deliver products that truly embody the organic spirit:

**Import and Export Regulations (if applicable):**

- **Understanding International Standards:** If you're involved in importing or exporting organic products, familiarize yourself with the specific regulations of the countries involved. The National Organic Program (NOP) website provides resources and guidance for US-based businesses navigating international organic trade.
- **Maintaining Documentation:** Maintain detailed records of your organic certification, import/export activities, and any relevant communication with regulatory bodies. It demonstrates transparency and facilitates smooth customs clearance.

**Food Safety and Quality Standards:**

- **Rigorous Testing and Analysis:** Organic products must meet strict food safety standards to ensure they are free of harmful residues and contaminants. Regularly testing your products through certified laboratories is essential for maintaining compliance and consumer confidence.
- **Organic Integrity from Farm to Table:** Make sure your supply chain is fully organic, from sourcing ingredients to processing, packaging, and storage. It ensures the final product embodies the true essence of organic and meets consumer expectations.

**Ethical and Fair Labor Practices:**

- **Treating Workers with Respect:** Organic certification standards often encompass ethical labor practices, ensuring fair treatment of workers involved in the production process. It includes providing safe working conditions, fair wages and working hours, and prohibiting child labor.

- **Building a Sustainable Future:** By upholding ethical labor practices, you contribute to a sustainable food system that values both environmental responsibility and social justice. It resonates with consumers who are increasingly conscious of the ethical implications of their consumer choices.

Achieving and keeping organic compliance is an ongoing commitment. Staying informed about evolving regulations, partnering with reputable certifiers, and building trust with your customers through transparency and ethical practices are all essential steps in navigating this complex landscape. By doing so, you'll cultivate a thriving organic business that contributes to a healthier, more sustainable future.

## Land and Property Rights

Owning or managing land is an exciting endeavor, but it also comes with responsibilities and legal complexities. Have the necessary rights and comply with relevant regulations to protect your investment and avoid potential pitfalls.

**Record-keeping for Compliance:**

- **Maintain Meticulous Records:** Keep detailed documentation of all property deeds, titles, permits, and other relevant documents in a secure and organized manner. It ensures easy access when needed and simplifies compliance with any legal or regulatory requirements.
- **Digitalization:** Consider digitizing your land records for easy retrieval and safekeeping. Cloud storage solutions or secure digital filing systems offer an efficient and readily accessible record management method.

**Keeping Up with Regulatory Changes:**

- **Stay Informed:** Land-use regulations and zoning laws can evolve. Regularly checking with your local government agencies or seeking professional guidance will help you stay informed about any changes that might impact your property rights or development plans.
- **Proactive Approach:** Staying ahead of potential regulatory changes allows you to plan effectively and avoid any issues arising from non-compliance with updated regulations.

**Legal Consultations and Advice:**

- **Seek Expert Guidance:** Consult a qualified land-use attorney for legal advice and guidance. They'll help you understand your rights and obligations, navigate complex legal processes, and ensure you are operating within the boundaries of the law.
- **Preventative Measures are Valuable:** Consulting a lawyer helps you identify potential land-related risks and develop strategies to mitigate them, saving you time, money, and unnecessary stress in the long run.

**Risk Management Strategies:**

- **Conduct Thorough Due Diligence:** Before any land purchase or major development project, conduct a thorough due diligence involving title searches, environmental surveys, and zoning verification. This proactive approach helps you identify potential risks and make informed decisions.
- **Plan for the Unexpected:** Consider purchasing insurance specific to landownership, such as title or flood insurance, depending on your location and potential risks. It provides financial protection in case of unforeseen events.

**Ethical Business Practices:**

- **Transparency and Communication:** Maintain open communication with neighboring landowners, local communities, and relevant authorities throughout any development or land-use projects. It breeds trust, and transparency, and minimizes potential conflicts.
- **Respecting Environmental Regulations:** Always adhere to environmental regulations and responsible land management practices. It includes obtaining necessary permits, minimizing environmental impact, and promoting sustainable land use.

Navigating land and property rights is a complex and nuanced area. Maintain well-organized records, stay informed about regulations, seek legal counsel when needed, implement risk management strategies, and uphold ethical practices. It'll ensure your land ownership journey is secure, responsible, and successful.

**Key Takeaways:**

- Understanding local agricultural regulations. Familiarize yourself with local zoning laws, land-use regulations, and any specific requirements for flower farming in your area.
- Prioritizing worker safety. Implement and conform to all necessary worker safety regulations, ensuring the well-being of your employees and creating a safe working environment.
- Navigating organic standards. If you plan to pursue organic certification, thoroughly understand and comply with relevant organic farming regulations and best practices.
- Securing land and property rights. Ensure you have the necessary permits and legal agreements in place

for the land your farm operates on, avoiding any potential land-use disputes down the line.

- Maintaining ethical business practices. Conduct your business with integrity, adhering to fair labor practices, environmental regulations, and all relevant tax laws.

Prioritizing compliance, seeking expert guidance when needed, and upholding ethical business practices to ensure your flower farm operates within the legal framework. It'll foster a sustainable and prosperous future for your floral passion. Building a strong team becomes crucial for continued success as your business grows. In the following chapter, you'll explore strategies for attracting and retaining talented individuals, fostering a positive work environment, and cultivating a team that shares your passion for flowers.

# Chapter 11: Building a Strong Team

"Coming together is a beginning; keeping together is progress; working together is success," Henry Ford aptly captured the essence of teamwork.

As your flower farm flourishes, the need for a dedicated and passionate team grows alongside it. This chapter empowers you to identify your staffing needs, create a nurturing work environment, and cultivate a team that thrives on collaboration and shared passion, fostering success for both your business and your employees.

## Creating a Successful Workforce

Your team is the backbone of your organization. They're the ones who bring your ideas to life, solve problems, and drive success. However, building a strong team isn't just about hiring warm bodies. It's about carefully identifying needs, nurturing talent, and fostering a positive work environment. Here are the essential steps to build a team that thrives:

**Identifying Staffing Needs:**

- **Recruiting and Hiring:** Go beyond simply posting job ads. Utilize diverse recruiting channels, network strategically, and screen candidates carefully to find individuals who possess the necessary skills and align with your company culture.
- **Effective Job Interviews:** Don't just ask generic questions. Design interview questions that assess skills, cultural fit, and problem-solving abilities. Utilize behavioral interview techniques to gain insights into past experiences and predict future performance.
- **Onboarding and Training:** Don't throw new hires into the deep end. Have a structured onboarding program introducing them to your company culture, values, and daily operations.

Provide comprehensive training so they excel in their roles.

- **Clear Roles and Responsibilities:** Clearly define roles and responsibilities for each team member, avoiding ambiguity and ensuring everyone understands their individual and collective contributions.
- **Positive Workplace Culture:** Build a culture of collaboration, respect, and open communication. Encourage teamwork, celebrate successes, and create an environment where employees feel valued and heard.

**Employee Retention Strategies:**

- **Performance Evaluations:** Conduct regular performance evaluations to provide feedback, identify areas for improvement, and acknowledge achievements. This two-way dialogue helps employees understand their strengths and weaknesses and motivates them to grow.
- **Competitive Compensation:** Conduct market research and offer competitive salaries and benefits packages to attract and retain top talent. A competitive compensation package goes beyond just salary and includes health insurance, paid time off, and retirement savings plans.
- **Perks and Benefits:** Consider offering additional perks and benefits that go beyond the standard package. It could include flexible work arrangements, wellness programs, or professional development opportunities. These perks show your employees you value their well-being and will contribute to a positive work environment.

**Workplace Safety and Health:**

- **Conflict Resolution:** Equip your team with conflict resolution skills through training and workshops. Encourage open communication and provide a safe space for employees to voice concerns and work through disagreements constructively.

- **Empowerment and Delegation:** Empower your team members by giving them ownership of their tasks and delegating responsibilities appropriately. It engenders trust and accountability, encouraging them to take initiative.
- **Team Collaboration and Synergy:** Create opportunities for collaboration through team-building activities, brainstorming sessions, and cross-functional projects. It fosters synergy, leverages diverse strengths, and leads to better decision-making.
- **Training and Development:** Invest in your employees' growth by offering ongoing training and development opportunities. It could include workshops, conferences, or tuition assistance programs. Helping your employees develop their skills improves their performance and demonstrates your commitment to their long-term success.

**Cross-Training for Flexibility:**

- **Celebrating Achievements:** Recognize and celebrate big and small employee achievements. It could be through public recognition, awards programs, or simply acknowledging their contributions in team meetings.
- **Managing Remote or Seasonal Workers:** If you have remote or seasonal workers, establish clear communication channels, set expectations, and provide the necessary resources to ensure they feel connected and productive.
- **Handling Disputes:** Establish transparent and fair procedures for handling employee disputes. It could involve having a dedicated HR representative or implementing a mediation process.

- **Legal Considerations:** Stay informed about and comply with all relevant employment laws, including discrimination, harassment, and compensation. Consulting with an employment lawyer can help you navigate complex legal issues and avoid potential pitfalls.
- **Employee Motivation and Morale:** Keep your employees motivated by providing them with challenging work, opportunities for growth, and a sense of purpose. Regularly assess their needs and aspirations, and create an environment where they feel engaged and valued.
- **Providing Growth Opportunities:** Offer opportunities for career advancement within your organization. It could involve creating leadership development programs, internal job postings, or mentorship opportunities. By providing pathways for growth, you demonstrate your commitment to your employees' long-term development and increases retention rates.
- **Building a Diverse and Inclusive Team:** Make a conscious effort to build a diverse and inclusive team by actively recruiting from diverse talent pools and fostering a workplace that celebrates differences. It leads to a richer work environment and brings together a wider range of perspectives and experiences, ultimately leading to better decision-making and innovation.
- **Staff Appreciation and Recognition:** Regularly express appreciation for your team's hard work and dedication. It could be through a simple thank you note, a team lunch, or a public recognition program.

Building a strong team is an ongoing process. Your team is your greatest asset. By investing in their development, create a positive work environment, and recognizing their contributions, you'll have a team that consistently strives for excellence, propelling your organization toward success.

**Key Takeaways:**

- Identify your staffing needs. Conduct a thorough analysis to determine your current and future staffing requirements, considering factors like workload, growth projections, and skill sets needed.
- Develop employee retention strategies. Implement initiatives that foster loyalty and engagement, such as competitive compensation packages, opportunities for professional development, and a positive work-life balance.
- Prioritize workplace safety and health. Create a safe work environment by prioritizing proper training, providing necessary protective equipment, and upholding all safety regulations.
- Embrace cross-training. Equip your team with diverse skill sets through cross-training programs, fostering flexibility, adaptability, and a sense of ownership within the team.
- Foster open communication. Establish clear communication channels, encourage feedback, and create a culture of open dialogue where your team feels valued, heard, and empowered.

By nurturing a strong and collaborative team environment, you'll cultivate a powerful force to propel your flower farm toward a thriving future. As the industry evolves, staying informed about emerging trends becomes crucial. In the final chapter, you'll explore exciting innovations, shifting consumer preferences, and sustainable practices that are shaping the future of flower farming, empowering you to stay ahead of the curve and navigate your floral journey with confidence.

# Chapter 12: Future Trends in Flower Farming

"The future belongs to those who believe in the beauty of their dreams," Eleanor Roosevelt once proclaimed, and the future of flower farming is brimming with exciting possibilities.

As the industry evolves, sustainability, innovation, and ethical practices take center stage, paving the way for a future where beauty flourishes alongside environmental responsibility. This chapter delves into the emerging trends shaping the landscape of flower farming, empowering you to stay ahead of the curve and ensure your floral dreams continue to blossom in the years to come.

## Sustainability and Eco-friendliness

- **Conscious Consumers:** Consumers are increasingly demanding eco-friendly flowers, driven by a growing awareness of the environmental impact of traditional flower farming practices. This shift towards responsible sourcing is forcing the industry to use sustainable practices like reduced water usage, organic fertilizers, and responsible pest control to meet evolving consumer expectations.
- **Urban and Vertical Farming:** Urban and vertical farming techniques are gaining traction, offering innovative solutions for growing flowers in space-constrained environments. These methods minimize transportation needs and land use, contributing to a smaller environmental footprint and offering opportunities for local communities to connect with flower production.
- **Online Platforms:** Online flower sales and subscription services are revolutionizing the industry by allowing direct sales from farm to consumer. It reduces waste generated by

intermediaries and provides greater transparency about flower origins and practices, empowering consumers to make informed choices aligned with their values.

- **Market Diversification:** Diversifying flower offerings beyond traditional favorites like roses and lilies allows for more locally-grown varieties. It reduces reliance on long-distance transportation and its associated carbon footprint, supports local economies, and fosters appreciation for the unique beauty of regional floral ecosystems.

## Organic and Biodynamic Farming

- **Eco-certifications:** Consumers seek out flowers grown organically or biodynamically, increasing demand for certified farms. These certifications independently verify sustainable practices, fostering trust and transparency within the flower supply chain.
- **Collaborative Networks:** Collaborative farming networks are emerging as powerful tools for growth. These networks connect farms sharing resources and knowledge, fostering innovation, problem-solving, and f sustainable practices across the industry.
- **Climate-resilient Farming:** Embracing climate-resilient farming practices like crop rotation, cover cropping, and water conservation allows farms to adapt to changing weather patterns and build resilience against extreme weather events like droughts and floods. It ensures long-term sustainability and protects livelihoods and communities dependent on flower farming.
- **Ethical and Fair Trade:** Fair trade certifications ensure ethical treatment of workers throughout the flower supply chain, resonating with consumers who value social responsibility. By prioritizing fair

wages, safe working conditions, and community development, flower farms can contribute to a more just and equitable global market.

- **Biodiversity Conservation:** Integrating pollinator-friendly plants and fostering natural habitats within flower farms promotes biodiversity and supports healthy ecosystems. It benefits the local environment and contributes to the long-term sustainability of flower production by ensuring the presence of vital pollinators like bees and butterflies.

## Regenerative Agriculture Movement

- **Soil Health Focus:** The regenerative agriculture movement emphasizes soil health and building fertility through composting and cover cropping. It improves soil quality and water retention, enhances plant health, and reduces reliance on chemical inputs, leading to long-term sustainability and reduced environmental impact.
- **International Flower Trade Opportunities:** New technologies and improved logistics open doors for exporting sustainably grown flowers to international markets. It broadens consumer choices, fosters cultural exchange, and creates opportunities for flower farms to expand their reach and responsibly contribute to the global economy.
- **Educational Resources:** Educational initiatives and resources equip farmers with the knowledge and skills necessary to embrace sustainable and regenerative practices. These resources range from online courses and workshops to field demonstrations and mentorship programs, empowering farmers to make informed decisions and adapt their operations for long-term success.
- **Industry Events:** Conferences and events provide valuable opportunities for flower farmers to

network, share best practices, and stay informed about the latest trends and technologies. These events foster collaboration, encourage knowledge sharing, and inspire innovation within the industry, paving the way for a more sustainable and vibrant future for flower farming.

## Research and Innovation in Floriculture

- **Supporting Local Movements:** Supporting local flower farms offers many benefits. It gives consumers access fresher, more seasonal blooms, reduces the carbon footprint associated with long-distance transportation, and strengthens connections within communities by supporting local businesses and creating opportunities for direct interaction with flower growers.
- **Predictions for the Industry:** Staying informed about emerging trends and predictions for the flower industry leads to long-term success. It involves understanding shifting consumer preferences, anticipating technological advancements, and being prepared for potential disruptions within the market.
- **Embracing Agility and Flexibility:** The flower industry landscape is constantly evolving. By remaining adaptable and adopting flexible farming practices, flower farms can better respond to changing consumer demands, market trends, and unexpected weather events or economic shifts.
- **Continuous Learning and Improvement:** Continuous learning is essential for flower farmers to stay ahead of the curve. It involves actively seeking out new information, participating in educational programs, and embracing innovative technologies to improve efficiency, sustainability, and overall flower quality.

## Preparing for the Future of Flower

## Farming

The future of flower farming is brimming with exciting possibilities. Flower farms thrive commercially by embracing sustainability, innovation, and a commitment to responsible practices and contribute to a healthier environment and a more equitable global flower trade. Sustainable flower farms are conscious choices contributing to a future where beauty and sustainability bloom together.

# Conclusion

This comprehensive guide, "Flower Farming for Profit," has been your companion on the journey to cultivating a thriving floral enterprise. From the initial setup covered in Chapter 1, where you acquired the necessary equipment and mastered transplanting techniques, to the future-focused insights in Chapter 12 on emerging trends like sustainable farming and innovative technologies, this book has equipped you with the essential knowledge and strategies to navigate every stage of your floral adventure.

As you undertake this rewarding endeavor, remember that the key takeaways outlined below are the stepping stones on your path to success:

**Key Takeaways:**

- **Establish a Solid Foundation:** Grasp the essential equipment, transplanting techniques, and meticulous record-keeping practices that form the bedrock of a successful flower farm.
- **Nurture with Expertise:** Implement effective watering, post-harvest handling, and pest control measures to ensure your blooms' health and visual appeal.
- **Develop a Winning Marketing Strategy:** Explore diverse marketing avenues like fostering relationships with local florists, hosting engaging farm tours and workshops, and developing a memorable brand and packaging strategy. A well-defined marketing plan is the gateway to reach your target audience and achieve long-term success.
- **Embrace Financial Responsibility:** Develop strong financial management skills through effective budgeting, meticulous bookkeeping, and insightful profit analysis. Financial acumen is essential for ensuring the sustainability and longevity of your flower farm.

- **Become an Advocate for Sustainability:** Integrate eco-friendly practices like sustainable farming methods, energy-efficient operations, and responsible waste management into your everyday operations. By prioritizing sustainability, you contribute to a healthier planet and gain the trust of environmentally conscious customers.
- **Expand Strategically:** Before venturing into expansion, assess your readiness, explore financing options, and conduct thorough market research to ensure sustainable growth. Strategic planning is vital before you plunge into the complexities of scaling your flower farm.
- **Develop Resilience:** Be prepared to identify, manage, and overcome potential risks and industry-specific challenges that may arise. A proactive approach and the ability to adapt will equip you to navigate unforeseen hurdles.
- **Cultivate Lasting Relationships:** Build strong customer relationships through personalized interactions, offering value-added services like workshops or subscriptions, and practicing effective communication. Genuine connections with your customers helps you build a loyal and supportive community around your floral enterprise.
- **Embrace Innovation:** Stay informed about and incorporate emerging technologies like automated irrigation systems and drones into your operations to optimize efficiency and enhance your farm management practices. Continuous learning and adaptation are essential for thriving in the ever-evolving landscape of flower farming.
- **Operate with Integrity:** Follow all legal and regulatory requirements to ensure responsible and ethical business practices. Building trust and operating with integrity is fundamental to your flower farm's long-term success and reputation.

- **Assemble a Stellar Team:** Identify your staffing needs, develop effective employee retention strategies, prioritize workplace safety and well-being, and build a collaborative and supportive work environment. A dedicated and talented team is an invaluable asset for any successful flower farm.
- **Stay Future-focused:** Embrace emerging trends like sustainable farming practices, innovative technologies, and continuous learning to ensure your flower farm thrives in the industry's ever-changing landscape. A forward-thinking approach will position you for success in the years to come.

The success of your flower farm hinges not only on technical expertise but also on your passion, dedication, and willingness to learn and adapt. With the knowledge and strategies you've learned from this book, you are now well-equipped to cultivate a thriving floral haven, bringing joy and beauty to your community while pursuing your entrepreneurial dreams. So, step forward with confidence, embrace the challenges and rewards that lie ahead, and watch your floral aspirations blossom into a flourishing reality.

# References

*Bountiful Harvest*. (n.d.). FasterCapital. https://fastercapital.com/keyword/bountiful-harvest.html

*Budgeting for the first year flower farmer*. (2021, January 19). Sierra Flower Farm. https://www.sierraflowerfarm.com/blog/2021/1/19/budgeting-for-the-first-year-flower-farmer

Favaro, J. (2016, January 31). *Customer Relationship Management Florist Shop Report*. SlideShare. https://www.slideshare.net/JoshuaFavaro/customer-relationship-management-florist-shop-report

Kahan, D. (2008). *Farm management extension guide MANAGING RISK in farming*. https://www.fao.org/uploads/media/3-ManagingRiskInternLores.pdf

Kulbhushan Grover, J. I. (n.d.). *Principles of Cover Cropping for Arid and Semi-arid Farming Systems | New Mexico State University - BE BOLD. Shape the Future*. Pubs.nmsu.edu. https://pubs.nmsu.edu/_a/A150/index.html#:~:text=Adding%20Nutrients%20to%20the%20Soil

*Marketing Strategy for Cut Flowers*. (n.d.). Small Business - Chron.com. https://smallbusiness.chron.com/marketing-strategy-cut-flowers-75433.html

Mengistie, B. T., Mol, A. P. J., & Oosterveer, P. (2017). Governance of agro-pesticide through private environmental and social standards in the global cut flower chain from Ethiopia. *Ambio*, *46*(7), 797–811. https://doi.org/10.1007/s13280-017-0914-x

Muneeb Ahmad Wani, Din, A., Imtiyaz Tahir Nazki, Rehman, T. U., Al-Khayri, J. M., S. Mohan Jain, Raiz Ahmed Lone, Bhat, Z. A., & Mushtaq, M. (2023). Navigating the future: exploring technological advancements and emerging trends in the sustainable ornamental industry. *Frontiers in Environmental Science*, *11*(11). https://doi.org/10.3389/fenvs.2023.1188643

Seguin, R. (2022, May 3). *Small-scale flower farming as a form of environmental responsibility*. Www.floraldaily.com. https://www.floraldaily.com/article/9423808/small-scale-flower-farming-as-a-form-of-environmental-responsibility/

*Sustainable Flowers*. (2019, December 3). Sustainability. https://sustainability.wustl.edu/resources/event-greening-2/sustainable-flowers/

to 2023, D. V., HomeTips © 1997. (2012, July 11). *How to Choose, Grow & Care for Flowers*. HomeTips. https://www.hometips.com/diy-how-to/flower-care-maintenance.html

torriemeidell. (2022, March 9). *How to Start a Small Backyard Flower Farm (from scratch!) for around $200*. I Dream of Acres. https://idreamofacres.com/2022/03/09/how-to-start-a-small-backyard-flower-farm-from-scratch-for-around-200/

www.ingramcontent.com/pod-product-compliance
Lightning Source LLC
La Vergne TN
LVHW020117090726
842905LV00041B/1076